Turn Your Speaking into Cash

Branding & Marketing Your Expertise

Judi Moreo

Las Vegas, Nevada 89120
United States of America

Copyright 2019 by Turning Point International
All rights reserved

No portion of this book may be reproduced in any form or by any means without permission in writing from the publisher, except for the inclusion of brief quotations in a review.

Cover design and typesetting: Jake Naylor

ISBN-13: 978-0-9968817-9-1

3315 E. Russell Road, Ste. A4-404
Las Vegas, Nevada 89105
(702) 283-4567

Published in the United States of America

Disclaimer

This book is designed to provide information on promoting yourself as a speaker and obtaining bookings. It is sold with the understanding that the publisher and author are not engaged in rendering legal, accounting, or other professional services. If legal or other expert assistance is required, the services of a competent professional should be sought.

It is not the purpose of this book to reprint all the information that is otherwise available to speakers, but instead to complement, amplify, and supplement other texts.

You are urged to read all the available material, learn as much as possible about marketing your speeches and yourself, and tailor the information to your individual needs.

Every effort has been made to make this book as complete and as accurate as possible. However, there may be mistakes, both typographical and in content. Therefore, this text should be used only as a general guide and not as the ultimate source of marketing and selling your speeches and yourself. Furthermore, this book contains information that is current only up to the printing date.

The purpose of this book is to encourage and educate. The author and Turning Point International, Inc. shall have neither liability nor responsibility to any person or entity with respect to any loss or damage caused, or alleged to have been caused, directly or indirectly, by the information contained in this book.

If you do not wish to be bound by the above, you may return this book to the publisher with your receipt for a full refund.

Foreward

All novice speakers have the same question: "How do I get booked?"

Every intermediate speaker asks, "How can I get booked more?"

Every seasoned speaker asks, "How can I get booked for higher fees?"

Judi Moreo was a pioneer in the speaking business, as we now know it. In Las Vegas, she built a successful business, and through her skill, reputation, and relationships, she parlayed that into a successful speaking career that has spanned decades on several continents.

She is also the author of 11 books, including two international bestsellers: *You Are More Than Enough* and *Ignite the Spark*. She is the editor of *Choices* magazine, host of *Choices* podcast, and host of Armount TV's *The World of Book Reviews*. Her business awards are too numerous to list here.

Influential Las Vegas executives have been known to say, "If you want the impossible done, call Judi Moreo."

Remember, Judi built her business before social media, before LinkedIn, before websites, and before contact management systems. If you want to learn how to develop a speaking career and get paid, you would be well-served to take advantage of Judi's seasoned, practical, and tell-it-like-it-is, no-holds-barred approach. Judi has stayed in demand and relevant as a speaker and book coach.

I have looked up to Judi since the early '80s when I was new in my speaking career, and she has always been generous with her advice.

Her contribution to the National Speaker's Association in her local community is legendary, which is why NSA Las Vegas named their most prestigious award for her, "The Judi Moreo Achievement Award."

This book answers the questions you have about getting booked as a professional speaker. You will also learn the answers to questions you haven't even considered asking. *Turn Your Speaking Into Cash: Branding and Marketing Your Expertise* is put together as an easy, practical guide that is enjoyable to read.

Patricia Fripp, CSP, CPAE
Past President, National Speakers Association
President, A Speaker For All Reasons

About the Author

Judi Moreo, CSP

Judi Moreo is an award-winning speaker, author, trainer, and coach. She has presented keynote speeches, workshops, and seminars in twenty-nine countries on four continents. Judi Moreo is a Certified Speaking Professional. This is the highest earned designation in the National Speakers Association. At present, fewer than 12% of the speakers in the world have earned this designation. Judi's high quality, high content, high energy programs are well researched and delivered in a down-to-earth style that everyone will remember.

Prior to becoming a full-time professional speaker, Moreo was a successful entrepreneur. In 1986, the Las Vegas Chamber of Commerce honored her as Woman of Achievement – Entrepreneur. In 1992, she became an executive in one of South Africa's most prestigious media groups during the abolition of apartheid where she learned firsthand what it takes to be successful amid, political, social, and cultural differences. Today, she lives in Las Vegas, Nevada and serves as President of Turning Point International, Inc.

Judi has served on the Boards of Directors of the Las Vegas Chamber of Commerce Women's Council, the Las Vegas Professional Speakers Association, the World Modeling Association, the International Association of Model Agents, the National Speakers Association – Las Vegas Chapter, the Las Vegas Advertising Federation and Women in Communication.

The American Women in Radio and Television awarded her their "Outstanding Achievement and Community Service Award." In 2003, the U.S. Business Advisory Council named her "Nevada Businessperson of the Year" and the Las Vegas Chamber of Commerce twice presented her company, Turning Point International, with a Circle of Excellence Award. In 2004, she received the Diamond Star "Las Vegas Visionary Award."

While in South Africa, she was named, "South Africa's Most Outstanding Speaker," and in 2012, she was named one of America's Top 10 speakers by the eWomen network. In 2017, 2018, & 2019 her training and development company received the Best of Henderson award and in 2019, became listed in the Business Hall of Fame.

Judi offers workshops on writing and speaking as well as private coaching.

Her passion for living an extraordinary life is mirrored in her zeal for helping others realize their potential and achieve their goals.

For information on her coaching, classes, workshops, and other books, contact Judi Moreo at (702) 283-4567 or by email at judi@judimoreo.com

Client Endorsements

"Thank you, Judi, for making my speaking career not only possible, but meteoric! From the time you focused your outstanding coaching talents and instincts on my career, it has risen straight up. Your advice has proven to be excellent on all counts. Where I had nothing, I now have steady bookings as a motivational speaker and trainer. I look forward to reaching even greater success with your steady experienced hand on the helm."

    Bob Walker
    Salvage Master Productions LLC

"Rut buster! That's what Judi Moreo is. I have seen her deliver many different programs and the results are always the same, the audience is given many tools to bust out of their ruts and move up the ladder of success. Judi's style is very smooth and real. She tells you such great stories, because she has been down in the trenches. She has survived about 3 lifetimes worth of events so far in hers. Great stories. Great energy. Judi has helped change my life and I have seen her change many others.

    Frank Keck
    Author/Speaker/Business Coach

Judi has a vast experience in professional speaking and has written a number of good books relating to the self-help industry. She has traveled extensively and brings all of her experiences to her work. Judi will be around a long time spreading her talents across the range of self-help outlets. Do yourself a favor and either hire her as a speaker or take the time to come to one of her seminars and hear her speak!

>   Jesse Ferrell
>   International Speaker, Life & Corporate Coach
>   JessTalk Speaking & Coaching Firm

"Judi is a consummate professional! The ultimate "Class Act!" She inspires individuals, teams and organizations and provides them with concrete skills they need to achieve their ultimate potential. Whether you grow from one of her fabulous books or develop your success through her exciting keynote speeches and workshops, you will agree that Judi is one of the world's leading experts in self-development."

>   Dr. Casey McNeal
>   Speaker/Author/Business Coach

"What I like about her coaching is that Judi builds on my strengths instead of forcing her ideas and formulas. She coaches with a very positive attitude and that encourages me to work hard. The most important part is that she believes in me."

>   Paul Noor
>   Civil and Structural Engineer

"Judi is joyful, tenacious, driven by vision, committed to purpose and open to possibilities ~ especially open to possibilities. But what I honor and value most is that she always has a hand out to bring someone else along for the ride. I think the smartest thing anyone could do is to hire Judi or become her friend ~ my world is a better place because I know her."

>   Gail Cohen
>   Power Seminars LLC,
>   53 New Ocean St., Swampscott, MA

"Authenticity, tenacity, and integrity are embodied in Judi Moreo. She is one of the rare individuals that has a depth and breadth of expertise in every area that she writes, speaks and coaches about! She is without peers in the arenas of personal empowerment and growth!"

>   Courtney E. Anderson, JD, MBA
>   Attorney, Keynote Speaker, Television Legal & Business Analyst; Adjunct Associate Professor, Graduate School of Management and Technology, University of Maryland

"Judi Moreo has a heart of gold, wherever she presents, people are touched as much by her empathy, heart, and caring as they are with her exemplary knowledge. She can be counted on to respect others' time, provide them with more than they asked for, and follow-up on recommended performance initiatives. She is a jewel to work with, and a friend to cherish."

>   Micki Holliday, Director of Faculty and Curriculum
>   Rockhurst University Continuing Education

"Judi is EXTRAORDINARY in every way. Judi started to work with me in South Africa as a guest speaker over 15 years ago. The message she delivers is always sincere, relevant, and ignites her audiences. On a personal note, Judi has been an inspiration as a mentor and coach with great ideas and the tools to make things happen."

    Merle Whale
    President, Mbizo Events

Table of Contents

Is Public Speaking Actually A Business?	1
What Is A Brand And How Do I Create One?	5
How Can I Get Noticed?	9
What Should Be My Business Model?	11
Do I Have To Be An Expert?	15
How Do I Choose A Title?	17
Who Will Write My Introductions?	19
What Should I Do To Minimize Disasters?	21
What Makes A Speech Unforgettable?	23
Where Will I Find Clients?	27
Who Should I Talk To?	31
How Do I Get Credibility?	33
What's The Best Way To Advertise My Services?	35
If I Don't Have Referrals, What Can I Do?	37
What Are The Elements Of An Effective Letter Of Introduction?	43
How Do I Go About Making A Cold Call?	47

Should I Do Networking?	53
Can I Get Booked From Doing Social Media Marketing?	55
How Much Is Enough?	57
What Promotional Materials Do I Need?	59
Must I Have A Website?	61
What Goes On A Demo Video Or Sizzle Reel?	65
What Is A One Sheet?	67
What Is Meant By Article Reprints?	71
What Information Do You Put On A Menu Of Services?	73
What Is The Purpose Of A Pre-Program Questionnaire?	75
Should I Give Instructions On How To Set Up The Room For Me?	79
Should I Put My Contact Information On Hand Out Materials?	83
What Kind Of Evaluation Sheets Should I Use?	85
Do I Need To Send Out A Newsletter?	87
Do Speakers Still Use Business Cards, Thank You Notes, & Greeting Cards?	91
Should I Put My Picture On My Promotional Materials?	93
Should I Work With A Speaker Bureau?	95

Should I Send Gifts To Meeting Planners And Bureaus?	97
What Is A Speaker Showcase And Should I Do Them?	99
How Do I Track My Business?	101
How Do I Get Information About The Groups Which Hire Me?	103
How Much Should I Invest In My Career?	105
Should I Hire Someone To Do Public Relations For Me Or Should I Do It Myself?	111
How Much Will I Make As A Paid Professional Speaker?	115
How Will I Get Paid?	121
What Regular Expenses Will My Business Require?	123
Should I Have Products To Sell?	127
How Do I Get Products To Sell?	129
Why Would Someone Buy My Products?	131
What Should I Know About Seminar Companies?	137
What About Presenting Seminars On My Own?	139
How Do I Get Names Of People Who Might Want To Attend My Seminars, Hire Me To Do A Speech, Or Buy My Products?	143
Should I Join A Speakers' Organization?	145

Are There Other Professional Organizations To   153
Which I Should Belong?

Should I Have A Personal Coach?   155

Do I Have What It Takes?   157

Appendix

Glossary   163

Life Affirming Resources   169

Turn Your Speaking into Cash

Branding & Marketing Your Expertise

By Judi Moreo

Does the thought of marketing yourself for speaking engagements give you anxiety attacks? Do you dream of speaking on big stages, but fail to reach out to meeting planners because you aren't sure how to sell yourself? Do you feel if you call possible clients and tell them what you can do for their conference or business you are being braggadocious?

Who This Book Is For:
This book is written primarily for people who are either getting started in their speaking careers or people who are not getting the number of bookings they want.

The idea is to give you a quick, easy way to find some engagements and continue to do so on a regular basis. The goal is to ensure you don't feel any fear or hesitation when you are contacting potential clients.

This book is for people who have:
- a message that others want or need to hear
- put a program together in an entertaining and informative way, but don't know how to get into the marketplace
- delivered their message to non-paying audiences and are now ready to move into the paid arena

- tweaked their material so that it is understandable, concise, informative, and arouses emotion in their listeners.
- conquered the skill of speaking and want to be coached or mentored by someone who has been in the trenches and been highly successful.

In other words, this book is for people who are ready to enter the professional speaking marketplace, deliver a message that will make a difference in the lives of others, and get paid for it.

Who This Book Is Not For:
I often meet people who say they want to be professional speakers and then, upon speaking with them, I discover they just want to be on stage. They want recognition and to make a lot of money. In fact, they are still trying to figure out what they will talk about and to whom. If they have an idea for a program, they haven't put it together. Some of them have subject matter in mind, but have not organized it into an understandable, concise, informative style. Others think they know their subject, so they attempt to stand up and talk about it without proper preparation. This book is NOT for those people. They need to hire a speaking coach.

Get to Know the Speaking Community
The speaking community is a small one. People know each other. People know whether you are any good or not. And they talk! Everyone talks to everyone. And, they tell each other whether you are pleasant to work with. No one wants to work with a difficult person, and especially one who is a mediocre presenter. Therefore, you must know who you want to talk to, what industry they are involved in, what you want to talk about, and be

great at delivering your message. In addition, you must be agreeable to work with. If this is you, then continue reading.

In this book, I have listed the questions many people have asked me and answered them to the best of my ability. By the time you finish reading it, you are going to know exactly what to do. And, if you follow my directions, you'll never again need to be afraid of reaching out to meeting and event planners.

But beware! If you follow my instructions correctly, you may get more work than you know what to do with.

This book is not intended to be the ultimate training guide for speakers. It will address many of the important things to think about as you develop a business plan and set your goals. I am sharing information that I have learned from:
- my own successes and mistakes
- great mentors
- bureaus with whom I have worked
- observing other successful speakers
- speaker organizations
- reading articles, books and blogs from coaches, speakers and business leaders.

It is my hope that by having this information early in your speaking career, you will gain the knowledge and confidence you need to achieve your desired level of success.

Kindest regards,

Judi

Question 1

Is Public Speaking Actually A Business?

Yes, it certainly is, and you must always think and behave like a businessperson. You must identify what you are selling; why anyone should care: and be able to describe who you are and what you speak about in one or two words.

The place you occupy in the heads and hearts of your clients and prospective clients is what is known as "brand position." What do you stand for? Can you describe that in a few words? What do you do better than anyone else? What are the benefits the client will get from doing business with you?

Once you know what your message is and how you are going to powerfully deliver it, identify your target market. Who needs to hear your message and what benefit do you bring to the people in your audiences?

You must position yourself as an industry star. Set yourself apart with a few well-chosen words. Speaker, author, coach is not unique. You need specific words infused with results and emotional resonance.

Turn Your Speaking Into Cash

Example: *a dynamic, exciting, powerhouse with sensible information to instantly drive revenue.*

Clarify your value proposition. What do you have to say and why should they listen? Why do they care? Why do they need to hear your message? How is it relevant to current trends? Why are you the right person to deliver the message.

Your presentation must have a clear objective. What are you trying to accomplish? Is it to educate, inform, entertain, or persuade? Is it to inspire? Enlighten?

Wrap your message in a package the audience wants to buy. What does your appearance do for your brand? Do you look like the message you are delivering? There is a speaker in South Africa who talks about teamwork using an analogy of a pride of lions and how they work together when they hunt. He is always dressed as a game ranger when he speaks. His packaging fits his presentation.

Are you willing to commit financial resources?

Marketing, websites, sizzle reels, copywriting, graphic design, online and print production, public relations and wardrobe all cost money. You must be prepared to pay for these. So many new speakers tell me they will wait until they are making money as a speaker to get the tools they need. You can't wait. Get these things and get them paid for before you quit your 9 to 5 job. The day you enter the speaking market, you are competing against professionals. There are no paid speaking engagements for amateurs.

Judi Moreo

What makes you credible? Do you have expertise? Industry training? Certifications? Awards? Have you written a book or gotten a lot of media attention? Do you have a unique story like Captain Sully, the airline pilot who made the miraculous emergency landing on the Hudson River?

What have you experienced that allows you to reach out to others who need or want to know how you did it and are hoping to find out they can do it as well?

What are your strengths? Go back through your testimonials and see what people mention most about you. If you don't yet have testimonials, ask your friends and family what strengths you have.

Are you authentic? Are you real? Are the stories you are telling, your own true stories? People don't like phonies. You can't be one person on stage and another when you think no one is looking.

Focus on your essence (who you are,) your passion (why you do what you do,) and your uniqueness (what sets you apart from the rest.)

It's imperative that you set yourself apart. Your audiences need to engage with your brand and your presentations. What is unique about your point of view in your area of expertise? What is your innovative or creative approach to your topic? Are you and your brand so compelling and distinctive that people believe you are the only source for what you have to offer.

Turn Your Speaking Into Cash

You have a unique message and it must be delivered from your heart. Search back through your life experiences and lessons learned.

Question 2

What Is A Brand and How Do I Create One?

Where I grew up in South Texas, when people talked about branding, they were talking about permanently marking their animals by way of heat to indicate ownership of those animals. If our cows got onto the open range and somehow got mixed in with your cows, that brand would tell us which cows were ours and which ones were yours.

Today, branding is a marketing term meaning making identifiable a name, logo, slogan, and/or a design scheme with a product or service. As a speaker, you want people to readily be able to tell your message from someone else's message. So, it is important for you to create a brand....for your speaking and for yourself. You do this by distinguishing your name, your story, your purpose, your book, and your uniqueness.

But how do you do this?

Your branding position should answer the question "Why me instead of another speaker." Do not confuse this with a branding slogan.

Turn Your Speaking Into Cash

Example: *"An international speaker, best-selling author and noted authority on customer service."*

Slogan: *"When only the best will do."*

Your brand must be congruent, consistent, and comprehensive.

Congruent - Is your brand in keeping with who you are, your area of expertise and the audiences you want to reach?

Ask Yourself:
- Who wants what I have to offer?
- Who can benefit most from what I have to offer?
- Who can afford what I have to offer?
- Who is willing to pay me for what I have to offer?

Consistent – Be sure your message is the same throughout all your marketing avenues including:
- Speaking
- Coaching
- Consulting
- Websites
- Blogs
- Ezines
- Media
- Teleseminars
- Webinars
- Books
- E-books
- Articles
- Newsletters
- CD's
- Podcasts

- DVD's
- You Tube videos
- Apps
- Commercial and promotional products

Comprehensive – It is imperative that you create a positioning statement focused on your distinctive brand and target markets to convey how you can be of particular benefit. It must include:
- What you do (your expertise)
- Whom it benefits (target audience)
- A Hook (attention grabber).

A positioning statement helps bring clarity and focus to your marketing strategy and leverages your expertise to promote and grow your business.

Brand position *"An international best-selling author and noted authority on creative thinking helping individuals and organizations develop innovative strategies and products to become leaders in their field."*

Does your brand impart principles and values that will provide lasting and meaningful impact?

For example: *Disneyland and its themes of happiness, family, fantasy, and magic.*

Your brand should encompass how people feel about your product or service. Examples of people with strong feelings are the customers of Starbucks or Apple. You want to create this kind of loyalty. In the speaking industry, Jim Rohn had it. Tony Robbins has it. Brendon Burchard has it. Les Brown has it. Oprah has it.

Turn Your Speaking Into Cash

Your brand should be expressed authentically, and you should give your audience a reason to believe in you.

Your brand should be credible, and you should live up to whatever you say about it, and whatever you say must differentiate you from all the other speakers out there.

Question 3

How Can I Get Noticed?

If you want to stand out in the marketplace, there are many things you can do.
- Write articles for industry magazines. Magazines that are read by meeting planners are a great place for your articles. Don't insist on being paid for these articles. Give them to the magazines but insist they put a short bio and your contact information at the bottom of the article. Write about your area of expertise and show in the article how your expertise benefits their reading audiences.
- Speak to local chapters of national associations in order to get recommendations.
- Have a compelling, descriptive title for your speaking topic. Be sure the title includes the benefit to the audience.
- When submitting proposals or making cold calls, be clear about what the result is for the client
- At the end of articles and speeches, offer a call to action to invite phone calls and/or email inquiries to discuss your availability.
- Tell everyone you know that you are looking for speaking engagements
- Create a blog about your topic and promote it on social media and in your newsletter

Turn Your Speaking Into Cash

- Post on other people's blogs, make comments about their posts, and offer them articles on their subject matter
- Write a book on your area of expertise
- Make a demo tape of you speaking and send it to bureaus, corporations, and associations
- Make short videos on you speaking about your subject and post them on You Tube
- Look so good when you go in public that people wonder who you are
- Send out a regular newsletter
- Create an online magazine

This list should get you started. When you have done all these things, call me (702) 283-4567 and we'll brainstorm some more.

Question 4

What Should Be My Business Model?

The successful professional speaker must think of him or herself as a businessperson. Your speaking career is a business and should be treated as one. Yes, you are an educator and an entertainer as well, but most of all, you must be a smart businessperson.

Many speakers feel successful if they can fill their calendars each year with the same number of appearances as they did the year before. If they can add more appearances than the previous year, they believe their careers to be growing and thriving. They might possibly be earning a good living doing it that way.

My business philosophy is a bit different. I believe speakers are in the intellectual property business so we must learn to think in terms of both speaking AND residual income. While a speaker may increase his/her income by doing more or better paid bookings each year, the fact remains that it is the speaker who must personally fulfill the engagement in order to create the income.

We must think in terms of all the avenues by which we can deliver our intellectual property...books, ebooks,

Turn Your Speaking Into Cash

white papers, magazine articles, blogs, podcasts, audio books, teleseminars, webinars, training, and coaching. What if you became ill and couldn't go out and fill those appearances you have booked? How will you survive? How many products do you have? How many different streams of income? You must not only be consistently perfecting your platform skills; you must also be improving your sales and marketing skills as well as developing your product line.

With the increasing aggravation and inconvenience of travel, you may not want to be flying from one side of the country to the other day after day, week after week, month after month, year after year. Yes, it's nice to be in demand, to have a full schedule, and a long list of prestigious companies with whom you work. It is also nice to have one big client that books you for 100 days a year in your own city. Whichever way you do it is okay, if it makes you happy.

For years, I loved the travel, the exotic countries, speaking with people from new cultures, sleeping in wonderful hotels (and some not so wonderful ones) around the world, eating in fabulous restaurants and tasting new and exotic foods. My ego became very excited when someone was willing to fly me first class half-way around the world to speak to a group of people for 45 minutes and pay me handsomely for my time.

For five years, I worked in only two cities for two clients, five days a month each. I found that to be very satisfying as well. I got to know the people in my audiences, was able to tailor my material to their specific needs and see an increase in the clients' businesses and an improvement in their team members lives. I saw results!

Judi Moreo

That was very rewarding. Another client hired me to work 10 days a month for two years in my own hometown and that was fabulous, because I was able go home every night, sleep in my own bed and see my friends and family on a regular basis. In other words, I found all these different business models to be satisfying in different ways. They all fell within the category of paid professional speaker.

For many, the corporate or association client who pays a fee for your speech, workshop, seminar, or training program will be the goal. Corporate clients use speakers in-house for training and at conventions and seminars. They may want you to do an hour speech or a full day's training on a subject. Some corporate clients may employ you on a long-term contract to assist them in making improvements in their business.

Association clients will want you to speak at conventions or conferences to groups of people in the same industry. They may want you to do an hour keynote presentation, and/or a 3-hour workshop or a breakout session.

The profession is changing and a lot more programs are being offered using technology. If you are presenting material on-line through webinars or other technology, you are still a professional speaker, you are just delivering your message through a different medium. The diversity of the mediums we have available today almost guarantees you the opportunity to have a speaking career, and to build it in a fashion that is right for you.

Question 5

Do I Have to Be an Expert?

In the early stages of a speaking career, many speakers will take whatever bookings are offered to them whenever and wherever they are to take place, no matter what the topic requested by the client. They may even do a respectable job of putting together and presenting a credible program. However, if you are a jack-of-all-trades, you are less likely to get well-known in the marketplace. So, yes, become an expert. In fact, become THE expert.

Meeting planners are looking for speakers who are experts in a particular field. They want to know when they hire someone to train or entertain their employees, attendees or delegates, that speaker is the best qualified on the subject. It is best to speak only on those topics which you know something about, have an interest in, or are passionate about. You can become an expert on almost any topic if you are willing to devote the time and energy to research. You must always stay informed about new developments and information in your area of expertise and make sure what you deliver is relevant to your audience.

Look into your past. What have you done that qualifies you to be an expert in a particular field? Then build your

Turn Your Speaking Into Cash

knowledge in that area. You want to speak on topics about which you are an expert.

Corporate and association clients are usually looking for speakers in the areas of business and economy, management development, communication skills, new technology, self-development topics, future trends, new products and services, legal issues, stress management, health, fitness, and lifestyle. What do you know about any of these topics? How can you present one of these topics in a new way so that meeting planners don't think they are getting the same old program presented by a different voice?

Put on your creative thinking cap and see what you can come up with! The internet, creativity coaches, your local library, friends and associates are great resources for finding new ideas and new ways of presenting old ideas.

Question 6

How Do I Choose a Title?

Be sure you have a title that grabs attention. The first thing meeting planners see is your title. If it doesn't catch their attention, it's not likely they will read on and see what you have to offer. If the title is dull, flat and sounds like the same old thing, they will keep looking for one that offers something they can sell to their target audience.

The title is also your first exposure to your audience. It will appear in the event program or the agenda. If you are speaking at an event where there are several talks happening at once, your title needs to be intriguing enough to draw the people into your room instead of going to hear another speaker.

It is important to find a title that is interesting, unusual, and perfectly in tune with your speech.

At the suggestion of Joe Charboneau, I changed the title of my *"Dealing with Difficult People"* program to *"Look Who's Wrecking Your Company Now"* and increased the sale of that program within six months by 100%. People are intrigued by subjects that leave something to the imagination. You can imagine what this title brings to mind.

Turn Your Speaking Into Cash

You can also use titles that explain exactly what you are doing, "How to _____ So That You Can_____. You will, of course, fill in the blanks with what you are teaching and what they will be able to do as a result of your teaching. This is called a Benefit Title and is used more in trainings, workshop sessions, and breakout sessions than it is for a keynote.

Titles that list several reasons, secrets, or ways will work well because those titles make a very specific promise of what the audience will get.

Example: *Seven Habits of Highly Effective People*

Titles should not be too long. They should simply give the listeners an indication of what your speech will be about.

Make your speech title original. *How to Communicate Better* screams boring. Try something like *Effective Communication for Getting Through to Uncommunicative People.*

Be sure your title is relevant. It must have a relationship to the contents of your presentation. Audiences become very disappointed when the title promised information which they never actually heard in the presentation and they give you very low evaluation scores.

Your title is not as important as how you organize your material, deliver it, and engage the audience, but it will give you a competitive edge when meeting planners are making a choice of whether to hire you or someone with a dull and uninteresting title.

Question 7

Who Will Write My Introductions?

Write your introduction yourself. Write what you want it to say. It should explain why you are the right speaker for this audience. A week before your speech, send it to the person who is going to introduce you.

The person chosen to introduce you will not always be skilled in speaking in front of a group or in reading material they have not seen before. Give them an opportunity to be prepared so that the introduction will have the audience anticipating your presentation.

Call the introducer to be sure he/she got it and go over it with that person stating that it is to be read exactly like you wrote it as it sets up the material in your speech. Always bring a copy with you to the program – it may not be a priority to the person introducing you to remember to bring his/her copy along.

Be sure to speak with the introducer before the program so he/she is comfortable with the pronunciation of your name.

I learned the hard way to be sure I not only speak with the introducer but that this person has a written copy of my introduction in hand. I told the lady who was to introduce

Turn Your Speaking Into Cash

me, it would be easy for her to remember my name because it is Moreo...like Oreo cookies with an M in front. When she introduced me, not having a written copy in front of her, she remembered that my name rhymed with a word that had an "o" on each end and she introduced me as Judi Moleo.

Question 8

What Should I Do to Minimize Disasters?

Always arrive at your presentation destination at least an hour early. If something can go wrong, it will. You need to be prepared.

Find the person who oversees the room and check the SALT:
 Seating arrangement,
 Audio/Visual equipment,
 Lights, and
 Temperature.

If people aren't comfortable, they will lose concentration.

Also, check to be sure there are no scenic views that will distract the audience participants; that the coffee/food set-up and location are conducive to your product sales; where the elevators, restrooms and emergency exits are located; and what will be happening in the room next door.

You need to know what's happening next door because sometimes the noise is very distracting to your attendees. You need to be prepared to deal with just about anything,

Turn Your Speaking Into Cash

Once when I was working in Orange County, right in the middle of my training program, the hotel opened the wall which divided the large room into smaller rooms, and marched an elephant right through to the room on the other side of the room I was using. Had I known ahead of time that was going to happen, I could have scheduled a break at that time rather than having a disruption.

If you have a power point or other visual media presentation, be sure the format is compatible with the system they will be using. If you prepare your presentation in Windows 10 and they are still using XP, 98, or Mac, you may not be able to use it.

If you carry your own laptop, it is also wise to have a copy of your presentation on portable media (memory stick or thumb drive) just in case there isn't time between speakers to switch equipment.

If you use a Mac for your presentation, be sure to bring an adapter for the projection. Often time, venues don't have these adapters.

Question 9

What Makes A Speech Unforgettable?

Your speech needs to be full of impactful content. Start by asking yourself, "Who is in my audience?" "What do I know about their culture or the collective personality of the group? What are their wants, needs, and expectations? Why was I the one invited to speak to this group? What's the meeting planner's objective in hiring me? Always think about what's in it for the audience members to spend their time listening to you.

Customize your material to their needs, wants, and expectations. Be sure you can state the premise or objective of your presentation in one sentence. If you can't do this, it will be very hard for the audience to get your key message. Then, put in 3 to 5 main points of wisdom. Think of what stories, points, case histories, and quotes you will use to make your point clear to the audience. Use illustrations they can relate to. Use quotes from identifiable people. Always give credit to the person you are quoting. The audience needs to know who you are quoting. Use quotes from people in their industry. You can often find exactly the quote you need in their trade magazines. State facts which show the importance of the subject to the welfare of the audience.

Turn Your Speaking Into Cash

Open powerfully. Patricia Fripp, the first female president of the prestigious National Speaker's Association, says it this way, *"Come out fighting."* The opening and closing of your presentation have the most impact. If you don't hook your audiences' attention in the first 30 seconds, their minds are going to wander.

The body of your presentation will give nuts and bolts of your presentation. Have 3 to 5 informational points, followed by statistics and stories. Be sure to leave time for your close. One of the worst mistakes new speakers make is to give so much information in the body of the speech that they run out of time and can't deliver their close.

Your close should be the high point of your presentation, so summarize and answer any questions before you deliver your close. The last 30 seconds should send people out energized, fulfilled, and with a desire to do what you want them to do.

People remember most what they heard last and remember next what they heard first. That is why your opening and your close must be powerful and succinct.

Uniqueness is what makes you unforgettable. Ask yourself, "What is unique about my material? What is unique about me? What is unique about my speaking style? How can I best illustrate this uniqueness? Present with style, pizzazz, and enthusiasm.

Be authentic. Be real. Use stories and examples they can relate to.

Judi Moreo

Most fabulous speakers have a signature story. It's their story. It's a story that only they can tell. It would be almost impossible for someone else to tell that story.

For example: My signature story is about my brother. I talk about him as a young man, as a sailor, and then as a biker. I tell of the accident that almost killed him and the changes that were made by him and by our family because of his disabilities. I give examples of the relationships that were formed and the lessons he said he learned because of the accident.

No one else can tell that story...because he was my brother and it was our lives. I can deliver it with passion because I still feel the rollercoaster of emotions I felt back then. But it's not just a personal story. It vividly illustrates all the points I make in my presentation. A story like this is what makes your audience feel your authenticity.

Do people remember it? Yes, I get requests from clients to be sure to tell that story. I have people tell me 10 years later that the lessons my brother said he learned have stuck with them through some tough times. I have past audience members who call my brother by name and tell me they think of him often. Others send Christmas cards and tell me they keep him in their prayers.

One thing I really want to emphasize here. Be sure to get permission if you are sharing stories about someone else. I have my brother's permission to tell this story. In fact, it was at his suggestion that I tell it.

When I first started speaking, I used some of the old standard stories that everyone told. One day when I had to follow another speaker on the program, that speaker

Turn Your Speaking Into Cash

told all the stories I was going to tell, and he told them better than I could. During the break before I went on, I called my brother. As I agonized over what had just happened, he said, "Would it do anyone any good if you told them my story?" And that was my first standing ovation ... from 3,000 teenagers. The client has hired me again 23 times.

I have another story which is uniquely mine that other people have heard and copied, telling the story as if it is their story. I followed a speaker one day and I heard him tell it. After his presentation, I confronted him and he said, "Well, it could have happened to anyone." Perhaps it could have, but it didn't. It happened to me. He didn't even understand the point of the story. And he certainly wasn't as funny as I am when I tell it, because it was me who experienced the humiliation of being ignorant of the language. When it's not your story, you don't come across as authentic and one day, like this man, you will be caught out.

Examine your own life. You have lots of experiences that will make great stories. It is important to be real. A great authentic presentation is your payment to the audience for listening.

A good rule is one my mother often told us as children, "Don't speak unless you can improve on silence."

Question 10

Where Will I Find Clients?

There is an endless array of potential clients to speak for. Your contact person will differ depending on the type of organization that you are contacting.

Don't get overwhelmed. You might be thinking "Where do I even start? Choosing where you will begin looking for speaking engagements doesn't have to be a difficult job. Why not start with the internet? We Google everything these days. Doesn't it make sense that you can Google conferences and events? You can also search by industry, subjects, people, and titles. You can even do a Google search asking "Where do I get lists of (whatever type of industry or association you are looking for?)"

Once you get the lists, go to the websites of organizations and corporations in your local area as well as websites of national organizations. Look to see when and where their next events are being held and check to see if they have an application on-line for speakers for their event. If they do, fill it out. If they don't, contact them and find out who the event planner is and send a letter of introduction or make a call to her and ask when she will be taking applications for her upcoming event? Tell her who you are and how what you speak about could be of interest and helpful to the members of her audience. Ask if you may send more information or if she would like your website details. If she says yes, then do it right away. Don't let time go by before you send information as by the time she gets it she may have forgotten all about your phone call. Meeting and event planners are very busy people.

You can also set up Google Alerts. Set up the alert by putting in a keyword with quotation marks around it. Then, any time that keyword shows up on Google, you will get an alert in your email inbox. You can put in location or subject such as "Las Vegas Conventions" or "Franchise Conferences." You'll probably be shocked at the amount of information you receive.

There are literally dozens of places on the web to get lists like the Directory of Associations. You can get this directory free online, but it doesn't have the names of the people to contact. If you buy the hard copy or the email list, you will pay about $600.00 and it has the names and email addresses of the people you want to contact. This is an item that should go in your marketing expense budget. It's part of the price of doing business.

InfoglobalData.com has lists segmented by industry and positions.

Your local convention center will have a list of national organizations coming to your area for conventions. With most convention centers, you must purchase a membership in order to have access to the lists. In Las Vegas, we don't have to be a member, but then the list doesn't give you the name or contact information of the person you need to speak with.

You can also find potential clients on membership lists of business organizations. Join your local Chamber of Commerce, National Association of Businesswomen, Young Presidents Organization, Professional & Businessmen's Association, Soroptimist Club, Start Up Grind, Vistage, and Ashoka. These are just a few. As a member of these organizations, you will have access to the lists. If you Google Businessmen's and Businesswomen's Organizations, there are hundreds more.

Business networking events are a good place to meet people who can use your services. Every city and almost every organization has networking events. Don't be shy. Go to these. Meet people. Show an interest in them and their business and hand out your business cards.

Social media sites are a good place to meet business people, as well. We will address the subject of social media later in the book.

Remember, meetings are usually planned a year in advance. Even though you may be speaking a lot right now, you must be marketing all the time. This is not an industry where people do things at the last minute. The only time they do that is when someone cancels on them.

This recently happened to me. A speaker cancelled on a Friday for a program the following Tuesday. The meeting planner, who I had worked with about seven times, called me and asked if I was available and if there was any way I could speak on a specific topic which she had heard me do two years before. I pulled out the file for that previous engagement, looked at the mind map of that talk, re-freshed my thoughts, put in an up-to-date example and

Turn Your Speaking Into Cash

Voila! I showed up on Tuesday, presented the program, got a standing ovation, sold a lot of books, received my standard fee and slept at home in my own bed that night.

This doesn't happen that often. Smart speakers don't cancel on a client if it is at all possible for them to be there.

Question 11

Who Should I Talk To?

If you are approaching the **corporate market**, the higher up in the organization you can reach someone, the better. But getting through the gatekeeper (administrative assistant) is usually the toughest part.

I have found that if I call the office of the President, tell the admin who I am, and that I need a bit of help, usually this person will be most helpful. I ask if I should speak directly with Mr. President about it or is there someone else she would recommend that I contact? Most often, she will get me to the person I need to speak with and may even tell me about meetings they have coming up. If their organization doesn't use outside speakers for their meetings, the admin person will usually know this as well. Administrative Assistants to this level of corporate executive have a lot of power and a lot of knowledge. They can be your best friend or your worst enemy. Always be cordial and polite and be sure to thank them for any help they give you. If they are extremely helpful, send a hand-written thank you note.

I don't recommend that you contact Training Directors as they take your call as a direct threat. They think you are competing with them.

Turn Your Speaking Into Cash

If you are approaching the **convention and association market**, you want to attempt to reach the Executive Director. Once again, you may very well be met with a gatekeeper. The same applies here. Usually, you will be referred to a meeting or event planner. This person will gather as much information about you as possible and will then submit it to a committee who will determine the theme of the convention and decide whether you fit with their theme. They will read through the materials you send and often watch your videos on You Tube. If you send CD's with your Letter of Introduction and/or proposal, one of the members will probably take it to listen to in the car.

In many cities, there are convention service companies, event planners, destination management companies, and model agencies who subcontract work for conventions and associations and do the selection of the program presenters. If you have these in the city where you live, be sure they have your information on file. And if possible, get to know these people. Either go to their office, introduce yourself, and drop off materials, or attend association meetings of groups to which they belong.

Your local convention and visitor authority has a sales team who sell your city to the association market. It is imperative that you meet these people and let them know what you do. You will want to offer to do a free program for them. The more they know about you, the more likely they will be to recommend you to their association clients.

Question 12

How Do I Get Credibility?

Speakers need to be living examples of whatever it is they talk or preach. You must walk your talk, or the audience will not believe a word you say. The speaker who expounds upon the skills needed for a great relationship and who is personally going through a divorce or has kids who are drug addicts is not very believable. Nor is the one who talks about being disciplined and is 50 pounds overweight and smokes 3 packs of cigarettes a day. While they may make money quickly with their flash-in-the-pan philosophy, they aren't really in it for the long haul. Speakers reputations are based as much on their credibility as on their content and style. This goes back to being authentic and living your message.

However, speakers who have gone through a messy divorce or have kids who are in the juvenile justice system can speak about the lessons of their past and be able to shed light on what pitfalls to avoid to keep members of the audience from having those same issues. Someone convicted of home invasion can talk to audiences about personal safety and how to keep the crooks out. That is credible!

Turn Your Speaking Into Cash

When I was speaking at a conference in Copenhagen, there were three speakers on the program: a very successful car dealer from another country who was going to talk about how he became so successful; a blind man who was an inspirational speaker; and myself. We were seated at the head table in that order from the end. I was closest to the lectern. When the waiter served the entree of prime rib and vegetables, he put the plate down in front of the car dealer first, then he served the blind man, and just as he was starting to put my plate down, out of the corner of my eye, I saw the car dealer switch his plate with the blind man's plate. I was mortified. After the waiter had walked away, the blind man turned to me and said, "I guess he didn't like the way his food was cooked." Did the car dealer honestly think the blind man couldn't feel the switch of the plates? Did he think the blind man would never know? His manners were so bad that even a blind person could see how bad they were. And the point of this story goes even further, I was getting ready to move to the country where this man had his dealerships. I was in the market for a car. Do you think I would ever buy a car from this man? Who knows what he would sell me thinking I wouldn't know the difference? Talk about a loss of credibility.

Your behavior tells people who you are. You are always on stage. Your reputation travels the circuit of meeting planners and bureaus very quickly – good or bad. Remember, they talk to each other.

Question 13

What's the Best Way to Advertise My Services?

In the speaking industry, word-of-mouth advertising is the best you can get. When one person hears you speak, tells someone else how great you are, and that person calls you to do a presentation, you know you are on the right track. One of the ways I gauge how my program went is whether anyone came up afterwards and said, "I want to hire you for another program." If they didn't, then I need to review what I presented and how I presented it.

If someone calls you and says, "So and so, who hired you for a program last year, recommended you to me," then you are doing something right. If a client who hired you last year, hires you again, that's also a very positive message.

There are planners and bureaus who will not book a speaker unless they have seen the speaker live. Some believe that a speaker sizzle reel only shows a small snippet of a good presentation and the speaker may not be able to sustain that level of energy, personality, or knowledge for 45 minutes or a whole day. So, invite them to come and hear you. Or, ask if they would like a video of a complete presentation. They may surprise you

Turn Your Speaking Into Cash

and come or they may send someone they trust to hear you. Always speak as though they are in your audience. Sometimes they will be but haven't told you because they want to see who you are when you don't know they are watching.

If your speech was very good and the event planner liked you, ask her if she might make an introduction to another possible client. When I do corporate engagements, often there is more than one division or one department that can use my services, so an introduction from someone they know is very effective.

Keep a file on what you do for every client, because when they hire you again, you want to be certain of what you presented last year and/or the year before so you can make this program fresh and new.

If you're not getting referral and repeat bookings, you're not developing a long-lasting career. It takes a lot more energy to actively market to new clients for every speech than it does to prepare fresh, new material for an existing client or simply accept a booking your satisfied client has already marketed for you.

Question 14

If I Don't Have Referrals, What Can I Do?

The first thing is.... Look at your speech. Is it really, really good? Is it relevant? Is it informative? Is it entertaining? How can you make it even better?

The second thing to do is look at you. Are you easy to work with? Does your packaging fit their image? Do you take the time and make the effort to find out about their culture, standards, and members?

If you are new to the business and haven't done any programs that people can tell other people about or you need more work than you have booked at the current time, you will have to learn how to sell your program yourself through proposals, letters of introduction, response letters, cold calls, and social media.

Proposals are usually aimed at a specific corporation or association project. You may need to go to the potential clients' website and see if they have a call for speakers. If they do, you will probably do your proposal by filling out an online form.

Turn Your Speaking Into Cash

In most cases though, you will send out a proposal after you receive a request from a meeting planner. You have a program to sell and you'll be hoping the meeting planner chooses you as you will be competing with other proposals from other speakers.

In your proposal, always point out the benefits to them of hiring you to present your program. They don't care if you are the best speaker in the world if there is no benefit to their participants.

A **letter of introduction** introduces you, your qualifications, and/or your proposal to an organization for whom you wish to speak. You will include with the letter, information about yourself as well as demos of your speaking style and perhaps a book which you have written.

A **cold call** is exactly what it sounds like. You are going to pick up the phone and call someone who has probably never heard of you but has the potential to hire you. Many speakers will not do this. Some speakers hire someone else to do this for them. For me, it is better to do this myself. Who knows more about me and my programs than me? And, very often people are excited that you personally reached out to them.

A **response letter** is written whenever you are responding to a specific speaking request or a request from a bureau. In this case, you know the engagement exists, and you must convince the contact person that you are the right person to fill that need.

Judi Moreo

Example of Proposal (Put on Letterhead)

Proposal

Based on my understanding of your organization and audience needs, (speaker name) will provide a presentation on (title of program) for your (name of event) event which will be held in (venue, city, and state) on (date of event).

Presentation Title

Synopsis of Program

Bullet Point Audience Take-Aways

Pre-Event Preparation:
In order to understand the needs of your members and prepare relevant content, (speaker name) will:
- Send you a questionnaire to help with understanding event goal and audience needs
- Participate in pre-event phone calls with your planning team
- Send a speaker bio and photograph by (date) for inclusion in your promotional materials

At-Event Participation:
(Speaker name) will deliver a presentation at your event on the scheduled date and time as detailed in the "Event Overview" section of this proposal. (Speaker name) will attend any event sessions which you identify and network with your audience members. In addition, (speaker name) will attend any additional events such as receptions and dinners, at your request. We will discuss

Turn Your Speaking Into Cash

specific on-site expectations during our pre-event planning calls.

Post-Event Review:
Following your event, we will have a call to review your perceptions of the event and (speaker name) presentation. We ask that you share any feedback on (speaker name) presentation you receive from audience members. (Speaker name) will share any insights that might be useful to you for business development and customer retention purposes gained from discussions with your attendees.

Event Overview:
Based on our initial review of your requirements, we have discovered the following key facts about your event and (speaker name) presentation:

Name of Event:

Location of Event:

Title of Presentation:

Date and Time of Presentation:

In addition, it is understood that the following will be your primary event theme and message:

Event Theme:

Key Message:

(Speaker name) will customize her program, as needed, to fit the needs of (client name).

Judi Moreo

Equipment and Room Set Up Preferences:
- (Name of style) seating arrangement
- Lectern on Raised platform
- Lavalier microphone
- Projector: LCD
- High-speed internet access
- Screen
- Display table on stage, draped
- Display table back-of-the-room for product display

Any additional needs will be identified in our pre-event planning discussions.

Investment:

(Client name) will pay (speaker name) a fee in the amount of $XXXXX.XX + expenses to include air travel from (location) to (location), ground transportation, hotel, food, and gratuities.

(Client name) may record all or part of (speaker name) presentation if a master copy of the recording is delivered to speaker within 30 days of the close of event. (Client name) may distribute copies of (speaker name) presentation to internal staff but may not sell copies. Should (client name) wish to make other recording or distribution arrangements, a separate agreement will be required.

If you agree with the above, we will send you a Program Agreement.

Kindest regards,

(Your Name & Title)

Question 15

What Are the Elements of an Effective Letter of Introduction?

An effective letter of introduction contains three important elements:

The **opening** - This gets your reader's attention.

The **body** should tell the following:

- Your understanding of the audience and their meeting requirements. (Research them on the web. Their site will tell you when their conference is, who their customers are and what their business model looks like. You won't have to ask them. Convey you understand their business as well as their industry.)

- What you believe you can accomplish for them. Explain in one sentence why you are a match for their participants and the topic. Remember to always make it about them. Demonstrating that you "get it" is incredibly important. Don't tell them why you think you are the perfect speaker for them. They will figure that out if you can accomplish what they want accomplished.

Turn Your Speaking Into Cash

- Explain what your presentation is about and what the audience will gain from hearing you. Again, keep this short.

- You are not writing a resume here. Do not include any irrelevant information such as your marital status, the state of your health, or any details about your personal life.

- Include a link to your website and a link to a video that demonstrates your skills

The **close** thanks them for the opportunity to be their presenter and suggests a "next step."

The "next step" is also known as a **call to action**. Make sure to tell your contact what you'd like them to do next such as have a phone conversation with you, hire you for their convention; look at your website; or keep you in mind for future engagements. If you pose this in the form of a question, they will usually answer.

In today's market, your letter is usually an email. Be sure to keep it short and succinct. Busy people will not read long detailed emails.

Judi Moreo

Example Letter of Introduction

Re: Potential client event name, date

Dear _____,

Are you looking for a speaker who can knock the socks off your participants? Do you have attendees who need to know how to build better relationships with their clients? Do you want to make their time and your money well spent?

I have a presentation that has helped thousands of people communicate more effectively and become more successful.

By the end of my program, Knock Your Socks Off Presentations, your attendees will walk away knowing how to:
- Manage the Presentation Environment
- Get Attention Immediately
- Talk in Terms of the Listeners Interest
- Speak with Contagious Enthusiasm
- Deliver an Appeal for Action

You can find out more about me and what I can do for you on my website, www.yourname.com. Please check out my other Knock Your Socks Off programs.

I will follow up with you next week to see how we can make this your most exciting program ever.

Kind regards,

Your Name
Contact Information

P. S.

You can watch a quick 3-minute presentation here!

Turn Your Speaking Into Cash

Example Response Letter

Re: Potential client event name, date

Dear _____,

Thank you for your inquiry regarding my availability for your (name of event). I am available on (date of event) and will put a tentative hold on that date for you until we confirm all the details.

As per your request, I will be happy to call you on Tuesday morning at 10 am to discuss in more detail your requirements for my presentation and ascertain the information I will need in order to quote the costs for your investment.

I am looking forward to speaking with you and to the possibility of working with you to make this your best event ever!

Kind regards,

Your name
Your contact information

Question 16

How Do I Go About Making a Cold Call?

Picking up the phone and talking to strangers to try to get speaking engagements may sound terrifying, but it is a highly effective way to get business.

Adopt the mindset that you are not inconveniencing or bothering anyone. You already have a good idea that the people you are calling need speakers before you pick up the phone. Figure out who you are going to ask for, know what you are going to say, and dial.

Focus on the call. Forget about everything except the conversation with the person on the other end of the line. Know your objective of your call and stay focused on that.

If you get a secretary or administrative person on the line, tell that person who you are and ask for her help. She will know who you need to talk to in order to get a decision. Once you have the decision makers name, then ask to be connected to that person.

When transferred, if you don't reach a live person, leave a voice mail that says who you are, what you do, and you

Turn Your Speaking Into Cash

will be sending them some information at their email address or on their Contact Us form.

Remember, when you are on the phone, they can't see you so you can write out a script ahead of time and read it.

Sample Script:

"Hello, my name is ………………………… I am a speaker/trainer who specializes in……………………… Do you happen to hire speakers?"

If they say yes….

"Great. I don't want to take up too much of your time. I'd just like to get your email address so I can send you some information about my services, if that's okay."

If they say no…

"No problem… can you please transfer me to the voicemail of the person who does hire speakers?"

When you leave a message on voice mail, be sure to give the following information:

- Your name
- A way to contact you
- What you do (you are a speaker)
- What sets you apart (benefit to them)
- A close

Keep in mind that how you speak is as important as what you say. Speak as though you are a radio DJ or news anchor with a low, resonant voice. Be warm, genuine, confident, and quick. Don't leave a long drawn out message.

Remember, your primary goal is to move the process forward.

When you get the decision maker on the line, open the call with compelling material. You have less than eight seconds to get the listeners attention and interest him enough to listen to you. State who you are and your purpose for calling immediately, succinctly, and clearly. Be excited. If you aren't excited, the listener won't be excited either. If you believe in yourself and the value you are offering, you will be enthusiastic and more likely to turn prospects into clients.

Then ask questions. Some of the questions you will want to ask are:

- *What are the dates of your conference or meeting?*
- *What type of meeting is it?*
- *Do you have a budget for speakers?*
- *Do you make the decision on who the speaker will be or is that done by a committee?*

Listen to the other person's answers. People enjoy talking to people who listen well.

Then, describe your program, experience, and rates. Speak his language. Hopefully, you will have done your homework so you can talk about their organization in his terminology. Be authentic and answer his questions. Remember, speak with enthusiasm in your voice. Enthusiasm is contagious.

Turn Your Speaking Into Cash

Expect objections. The first thing most people do is blurt out a reason why it's not a good time to talk or a good idea. Simply relax, take a breath, and lead the call to the next phase.

It is important to know your value, so you can keep the conversation moving toward a partnership and the potential for working together on a future event.

Before hanging up, you will also want to know the answers to the following questions.

- *When will you make the decision on which speakers you will use?*
- *Where will the meeting be held?*
- *Do you have a theme for the meeting?*
- *What else would you like me to know about your group or your meeting?*

And it is always perfectly valid to ask for permission to send a demo or to ask for an email address where you can send more information.

If the conversation has gone particularly well, you might ask,

- *"Is there anything I can help you with right now?"*

Don't be afraid to ask for the business. If you know your objective and you have the decision maker on the phone, tell him why you are the best person for the job and ask for it.

If you've identified a client type which works well for you, it doesn't even require you do a lot of extensive research on the companies you will be calling. Often, it's enough to get the name of someone who might hire you, and a phone number. Gather your list before you begin, set yourself a quota for the day, and dial until you hit the quota.

Sometimes, you'll get a booking right away. More likely, you'll hear back from them months after making the call. Either way, by spending a couple of hours a week on cold calls, you will find it to be one of the fastest ways to start turning your speaking into cash.

If you are not comfortable asking for business on your first contact, then ask for permission to send an email with more information. Gathering email addresses over the phone and getting permission to send something is not nearly as intimidating as selling, and you'll have a higher success rate.

When you are selling to associations, you will sometimes find that the decision for who they are going to hire is made by a committee of four or five people. Try to get a conference call with the members of the committee. If that isn't possible and they ask you to send written materials, include a short video letter to them from you telling them who you are, what your presentation is about, and how excited you will be to speak with their group. Be sure to be enthusiastic and be packaged as well as you will be when you speak at their event.

Once you have a commitment from them, you will then send a speaker agreement and room setup and equipment requirement request. You may offer to do a video for them which invites their association members to come and see your program. You, of course, will not

Turn Your Speaking Into Cash

charge for this. It is a value added. Some speakers also offer to do a video to be sent to association members after the presentation. I like to have this one sent out about a week after people return to their office. It's just a reminder to act on what was discussed at the meeting. Another value added. Or, you could send a link to a webinar or teleseminar you do just for them.

Then, and only then, you may ask for a copy of their attendee list which you will use in the months to follow to maintain contact with the people who were in your audience and give them more value-added information. You may even ask them if they have used any of the information you shared and if it worked for them. If they tried something and it didn't work, you want to know that as well.

People do business with people they trust. Many of the attendees have the power to bring in speakers and/or trainers to their organizations. Once they know and trust you, you will have a better chance of getting more bookings. (And, remember, if a bureau booked you for the original booking, the bureau also gets a commission from any of this follow-up business.)

Question 17

Should I Do Networking?

Networking feels a bit like cold calling in that it is meeting new people who know nothing about you and telling them what you do in an interesting way. It is an excellent way to get leads, but nerve wracking to those who are not accustomed to doing it.

It is as simple as going to a Chamber of Commerce or other business organization meeting and introducing yourself as a speaker to others in attendance. Often, someone will want to talk to you after the event and ask about what you do and what your rates are. Be sure you have business cards to hand out.

Most people at events are as nervous as you are. Smile. Say hello. Introduce yourself. Have a good time. Don't be a salesperson. First, show an interest in them and what they do. Let what you do come up naturally in conversation. People are naturally interested in speakers and your exciting life, so have fun.

Be sure to get business cards and ask if you can email them with more information or add them to your mailing list to occasionally send them valuable information.

Turn Your Speaking Into Cash

Networking is worth the time and money it takes to do it. Making friends at events means that you'll be the person they think of when one of their own connections needs a speaker. Soon, people may start calling you, letting you know they heard about you from a friend of a friend Try to stay in touch with the people you meet, whether online or in person.

If networking doesn't seem to be working for you, change up the groups you are visiting. If you want to specialize in speaking for an industry, attend some association meetings for that industry. Find networking events where decision makers will be present.

Network with other speakers at the National Speakers Association or Global Speakers Federation meetings. Attend the meetings of the local chapters of these organizations as well as the national conference and meetings. Not only do other speakers attend, but many times bureau representatives or meeting planners will be there looking to meet new speakers. Speakers very often refer other speakers to their clients. Many of my clients use more than one speaker for each event. I love to recommend people who I know are good speakers. It makes me look good when they do a great job. And in many cases, the people I recommend are my friends who live in another part of the country or the world, and we get to see each other and spend a bit of time together at the conference.

Question 18

Can I Get Booked from Doing Social Media Marketing?

Social media is more about creating awareness than it is about getting bookings. You want to have a strong social media presence to keep your name in front of bureaus, clients, and potential clients. What do I mean by strong? Daily and several times a day.

While you can get speaking engagements on job boards, such as eSpeakers, they come with a lot of heavy competition. Often, you'll find yourself in a race to offer the lowest possible rates as you struggle to compete with other speakers all writing the same sort of letters.

Locating speaking/training engagements on social media is not an easy task, but it can be done. First, you must identify that there is a company with a need for a program such as yours. You can do this by using hashtags. Try these #Conventions, #Conferences, #ConferenceSpeaker, #BusinessEvent, #(Subject such as Real Estate, Educational, Marketing)Conference, #Conference (Location).

Before applying for any speaking engagement, "Like" their page, follow them on Twitter, and read some of

Turn Your Speaking Into Cash

their posts. Then when you write a letter, refer to one of their posts by saying something complimentary about what they have posted or point out things you have in common. It's important to create a connection before you attempt to sell them something.

One of the great things about social media is that it can put you directly in touch with decision makers.

Make sure your social media profiles are stellar. You want to present your professional best. This means you want a professional photograph and you make it clear what you do and your area of expertise. Link your profiles to your speaker website. Make it easy for potential clients to see at a glance who you are and what you do.

Use social media to give yourself an advantage. Post information that is useful to meeting and event planners, and potential clients about your subject. When you are at their events, take pictures of yourself along with attendees, exhibitors, or even the event planner and post on Social Media. When they see you are posting about their event, it will remind them of you and how great you were to work with.

Question 19

How Much Is Enough?

Now that you know what to do and where to do it, you need to ensure you are reaching out to enough people to fill up your speaking calendar and bring in the work. But how much is enough?

Everyone's answer will be different. Much will depend on:
- The types of companies/organizations with whom you are looking to work
- How effective you are at sales & marketing
- How much work you get from any one client?
- The number of repeat clients you get

When you are first starting out, you can use the following plan to help you fill up your calendar quickly:
- Make twenty-five cold calls a day. That means you'll make 125 a week, or 500 in a month. Even if you're bad at cold calling, you will almost certainly land anywhere from five to twenty-five clients by doing this.
- Send out at least fifteen cold letters a week. These are letters of introduction. That means you'll mail out sixty letters your first month. The odds of landing a client or two are pretty good.

Turn Your Speaking Into Cash

- Spend an hour or two each week searching the web for associations with a call for speakers, filling out their forms, and sending letters of introduction.
- If you like the idea of using social media as a marketing method, then you can spend an hour each day joining groups, responding on those groups, and following up on leads.

As your calendar fills up, you may cut back these efforts because you'll be spending your time on bookings. Just make sure you don't abandon these techniques all together. You never know when clients will leave you, or you will run out of work. You don't want to find yourself in a panic or a financial bind when this happens.

The good news is you always have the option to send out more letters of introduction. The more you send, the more clients you'll get...it's that simple. If you are having a slow day, week, or month, there's no need to stare at your inbox, hoping some work will magically appear. You can always stay productive by getting busy and finding more work.

Your efforts will be rewarded if you're making the effort to contact corporate and association executives effectively. You can't just send out hundreds of generic pitches or make tons of fruitless calls and expect results, but focusing your efforts and targeting the companies, and organizations that will be a good fit for you is a great way to improve your success rate. Sooner or later, you'll land some fantastic assignments. Present an awesome program for them and you'll be on your way toward a robust and lucrative speaking career.

Question 20

What Promotional Materials Do I Need?

When you enter any business, you must have a budget for marketing and promotion. If you don't market and promote yourself, how is anyone going to know you are here? It amazes me how many speakers don't invest in the proper promotion of themselves. In today's marketplace, your promotional materials will not cost you the fortune they did when I started out. Thanks to computers and the internet, you can promote yourself relatively inexpensively. But you do have to make an investment.

You will need the following:

1. Website
2. One sheet
3. Client list
4. Article reprints
5. Menu of services you offer
6. Biography (Bio)
7. Color photos – good quality taken by a photographer: Headshot and a full length shot.
8. Black and white photo – headshot
9. Pre-program questionnaire

Turn Your Speaking Into Cash

10. Instructions for room set-up
11. Postage paid mail back card and/or an online "contact me" form
12. Evaluation forms
13. Newsletter
14. Product brochure or catalogue
15. Hand out materials
16. Business cards, thank you notes and seasonal greeting cards
17. Demo CD or MP3
18. Demo DVD or Sizzle reel

The technology available today allows you to print high-quality copies of your materials and make copies of your CDs, DVDs, and MP3s as you need them. You no longer need to order and store 500 copies of your one sheet, your press packet or your demos to get a good price as we once did. You also have the freedom to revise, update and add to your promotional package as your experience, client list and career grows. And the best part, everything in your press kit can be sent digitally to clients and/or added to your website.

Question 21

Must I Have A Website?

A speaker needs to have a good website. This is the place where bureaus and clients can learn about you and see and hear a sample of your work. This is not a Facebook page or a LinkedIn profile. It is an actual domain that you own and should be www.yourname.com. That makes it easy for people to find you. Make sure your website looks professional. If it looks amateur, clients will assume you are an amateur. Unless you are a technical genius or a graphic artist, don't attempt to set up your website yourself. It is important to invest in hiring a professional web designer who knows the speaking industry to create your website. Jake Naylor 1 (858) 204-3954. jake@jakenaylor.com is who I use and recommend. In addition to being visually interesting and well organized, a good website should contain the following things:

1. Home page
2. Demo video (3-4 minutes in length) This could be the most important part of your website
3. A synopsis of each program you present
4. Menu of services you offer
5. Resources you can provide
6. "Working with me" page
7. Testimonials from clients and client logos – Testimonials are social proof that you are good at

what you do. If you have done a great job for an organization, don't be afraid to ask the decision maker to send you a testimonial. Often, they will send it to you without being asked, but there is no harm in asking.
8. Pre-program questionnaire
9. Sample bios and introductions
10. Promotional photos – a good headshot and several pictures of you speaking before an audience
11. Room and A/V requirements
12. Association memberships and/or logos, any certifications and degrees
13. Newsroom or Media room
14. Blog
15. Contact information – This should be on every page of your website.
16. Links to social media

There was a time when some bureaus required that you also had a bureau-friendly website. This means you don't have your personal contact information on the site. In this way, the bureau can link to your site, send their clients over to look at you and your video and have some assurance that the client will come back to them when they want to hire you. It didn't work out too well. If a client wants to find you on the web, they can. The important thing is for you to be honest. Work with the bureau whenever you can. The more you work with them and they make commissions from you, the more they will book you.

Many of my coaching clients have asked me to write up their promotional materials for them as they have great difficulty in writing about themselves. If that is the case with you, hire someone to help you write up your materials. Once they are written, you can tweak and update them regularly.

You must invest in yourself, if you are to be successful. As a business, you will have startup costs but not nearly what you would have in many other businesses and you will break even relatively quickly.

Question 22

What Goes on A Demo Video or Sizzle Reel?

Before bureaus are willing to represent you and decision makers are willing to invest, they want to get a sense of how you present and who you are. Think of this as a movie trailer... it just shows the highlights, gives them an overview of who you are and what you do, and hopefully, will make them want to see and hear more. This should be very much like your speech. It will have an opening, a body, and a close.

The opening is the first 60 seconds of your video. It must quickly capture the attention of the person watching. Open with something exciting enough to make them want to keep watching.

The body is the next 2 minutes which shows you speaking to a group making the main points that you make in your presentations along with your examples which drive the points home. This should be some of your most powerful material.

Then put in 1 minute of testimonials from others. You can get these by quickly videoing some of your audience participants right after they've heard you speak. It's

Turn Your Speaking Into Cash

important that they say something specific they got from your program and how they feel that will make a difference in their lives. It is okay to coach them to say what they are going to say in a most effective manner.

The last minute of the demo should show you interacting with members of your audience and it should give your website, phone number, and email. Or you can individualize these for bureaus and give their contact information.

Remember what I told you earlier, the close of any presentation is what people remember the longest, so you want the closing to be powerful. You want them to think, "Wow. That was great. I have to hire this person, right now!" If your video doesn't do that, keep working on it until it does. Don't send out a mediocre video.

Also, this video should be right at the top of the first page of your website. You want people to look at it without having to scroll anywhere else and it should be so exciting it makes people want to look at the rest of your website.

Question 23

What Is a One Sheet?

One sheets may seem a bit old fashioned as they are the one piece of promotional material speakers have been using for years. However, they are as important today as they have always been.

A one sheet consists of a professional headshot, your positioning statement, a brief bio, speech title and synopsis including what you can do for the client and bullet points of audience take-aways, testimonials from clients, and contact information.

Because people like visuals, be sure to have a couple of pictures of yourself in action, your client's logos and the logos of any professional organization to which you belong such as the National Speakers Association or the Global Speakers Federation. While Toastmasters is an excellent place to learn and practice speaking skills, it is not recognized as an organization of professional speakers, so you may not want to put their logo on your professional marketing materials.

Be sure to provide each bureau that represents you with one sheets that have the bureau contact information instead of your own. Bureaus need these in their possession to mail or email to prospective clients. In

Turn Your Speaking Into Cash

addition, the bureau marketing persons often use them as a script when doing sales because the one sheets have enough information on them to make the marketing people sound like they know you personally.

You can also have one sheets as the last page of your handouts, put them on your product table and include one in all sale of product. It is also very smart to put a one sheet on the attendee seats in all presentations. This way, they can learn about you while waiting for you to speak and take with them assuring they have your name and contact information.

Judi Moreo

Example One Sheet

Judi has inspired hundreds of thousands of people around the globe with her unique speaking and training style.

Become Engaged in Learning with Immediate Application

Because you want your attendees to be totally engaged in learning how to apply immediate, applicable skills that will positively affect their relationships, both personally and professionally, you need to have Judi Moreo speak to your group.

Judi has all the elements that you look for in an expert speaker: knowledge, experience, high energy, humor, creditability, and customized content.

She is the expert you want because Judi:

- Brings a fresh perspective to inspire those who feel stuck
- Challenges and motives people to be their best selves
- Ignites and empowers attendees to improve performance
- Promotes the importance of teamwork and how to make it work for them
- Helps them discover how to open doors to bring greater success to their careers, relationships, and their lives.

Key Insights for Business & Personal Growth

Judi offers key insights for business and personal growth, collaboration, and finding new paths to improvement. Coming from an expansive professional background in the corporate environment, the international marketplace, and as an entrepreneur, Judi stands alone as one of the top speakers in the world while sharing her own story of success.

"Inspiring"
"If you're planning an event and want an inspiring, adventurous, poignant, and witty speaker, you certainly couldn't possibly find anyone who would please you more."
Judy Lawton
Founder and CEO, The Lawton Group

"Effective"
"The response to Judi's talk superceded my wildest expectation. Without exception, all delegates verbalized appreciation of her message, but more importantly, we have been able to take tangible hints to help improve our overall effectiveness."
Cliff Sclanders
Sales Manager
DHL Worldwide Express

"Extraordinary"
"Judi is EXTRAORDINARY in every way. Judi started to work with me in South Africa as a guest speaker over 15 years ago. The message that she delivers is always sincere, relevant and ignites her audience… Judi is an asset to everyone out there!"
Merle Whale, President
Mbizo Events

Judi's knowledge and expertise are powered by her passion for learning and delivered with humor and energy to provide programs guaranteed to enrich the lives of all who hear her.

Turn Your Speaking Into Cash

Example One Sheet (continued)

International Speaker

As a popular conference speaker, Judi Moreo has shared the international stage with many notable speakers and hundreds of the world's thought leaders and innovation experts. Here are some of the countries Judi has spoken in:

- United States of America
- Canada
- Bophuthatswana
- Botswana
- Egypt
- Kenya
- Mozambique
- Namibia
- South Africa
- Swaziland
- Tanzania
- Ecuador
- El Salvador
- Mexico
- Trinidad
- Hong Kong
- Indonesia
- Malaysia
- Singapore
- Thailand
- Belgium
- England
- France
- Germany
- Holland
- Switzerland
- United Arab Emirates
- Australia

"Powerful"
I heard Judi Moreo speak. Her message is powerful and yet was entertaining and humorous. The stories she illustrates gave a convincing impact to her message. I can't ever remember when I have been more impressed or enjoyed a speaker more."

Cavett Robert
Founder, National Speakers Association

"Sound Advice"
With sound advice to chamber leaders from a diverse background of 84 countries, Judi's session was one of our most popular workshops — standing room only."

Anthony Parkes
Director, World Chambers Federation

Judi's Clients Include

- AARP
- Alberta Hospital Association
- American Institute of Banking
- Belterra Casino Resort
- Blue Cross, Blue Shield
- BMW
- California State University
- General Dynamics
- Meeting Planners International
- Mutual Life Insurance
- National Association of Home Builders
- Nebraska Department of Roads
- Nestlé
- Pizza Hut
- Station Casinos
- Sony
- South African Police Department
- U.S. Army
- U.S. House of Representatives
- Walt Disney Imagineering

To Book Judi for Your Event

Remarkable!
A Speakers Bureau
Sue Falcone
888-766-3155

Question 24

What Is Meant by Article Reprints?

On your website, you should have a Media page and, on that page, post all articles that have been written about you in magazines, blogs, and newspapers as well as any articles you have written for any media. In addition, add links to any radio and television shows on which you have appeared. If you are going to put these in a physical packet to give to potential clients, you may either make a collage of articles like the one illustrated on the following page or make copies of the articles for inclusion. Be sure copies of any newspaper or magazine articles also show the name of the publication as well as the date and page number.

Turn Your Speaking Into Cash

Example Article Collage

Question 25

What information do you put on a Menu of Services?

You simply list all the things you are qualified to do:

- Keynote speeches
- Workshops
- Break out sessions
- Emcee
- Facilitation
- Consulting
- Coaching
- On-line coaching
- Webinars
- Podcasts
- Teleseminars

Speakers will often put the time parameters and prices for each of the services they offer on their menu of services.

Question 26

What Is the Purpose of a Pre-Program Questionnaire?

After you have booked an engagement, send a pre-program questionnaire to the meeting planner. Ask the meeting planner to answer the questions that he feels are important for you to have the information in order to customize your program to their audience. And to send it back to you with any other information they would like to share. I also ask for association and trade magazines, as well as corporate annual reports that are available to the public. The more you know about the client and their business, the better presentation you can do for them.

Pre-Program Questionnaire (should ask for)

- First & Last Name
- Company Name
- Address
- City
- State/Province
- Zip Code/Postal Code
- Country
- Phone Number
- Email
- Web Address

Turn Your Speaking Into Cash

The Program
- Meeting Date
- Length of Presentation
- Beginning Time of Presentation
- Ending Time of Presentation
- (Speaker's) Role ie Opening Keynote, Breakout Session, Luncheon Speaker, etc.
- Type of Meeting
- Program Theme
- Appropriate attire
- Program should be targeted to:
- Any key points (speaker) should address
- Three people (speaker) can call to familiarize herself with your organization
- Name & Contact Information of Introducer
- Names & Titles of Company Executives speaking before (speaker)
- Other Professional Speakers on the Program

Professional Speakers Used in the Past
What did you like about their presentations?

Audience Analysis
- Number of attendees
- Percentage male/female
- Age range
- Important changes happening in your industry/company
- Challenges and concerns of senior management
- Challenges and concerns of attendees
- Makeup of audience: Customer Service, Sales, Vendors

Company Information
- President/Executive Director Name & Contact Information
- VP of Sales & Marketing
- VP of Customer Service
- HR Director
- Training Manager
- Important changes in your company/industry
- Company/Association/Team accomplishments
- Company slogan/philosophy

Issues which should not be mentioned:

Logistics
- Nearest airport to meeting site
- Transportation to and from airport/meeting site
  ____ Meet (speaker) ____ Have (speaker) take a cab
- Hotel
- Location of Hotel
- Distance to Meeting Site
- Contact Name & Phone Number in case of emergency or flight delays

Are you interested in purchasing any of (speaker's) books for attendees?

Contact information for decision maker

Please send the following when they are available:
- The agenda for this meeting/conference
- Information about the company/organization
- Past meeting/conference brochures
- Copy of current trade magazine

Question 27

Should I Give Instructions on How to Set Up the Room For Me?

The room in which you will be presenting will determine how flexible the meeting planner and the venue will be in setting up the room the way you want it. Theaters often have permanent seating. Large halls can be set up in various ways depending on how many people will be attending. I ask if it is possible to set the chairs in a Chevron pattern. Often, I get it. Sometimes, I do not. In smaller rooms that are used for meetings and break-out sessions, venues are more adaptable. When I do Creativity programs, I ask to have round tables with either 8 or 10 chairs per table. If doing a seminar or workshop where participants will need to do a lot of writing, I will often ask for the room to be set up classroom style with tables and chairs.

U shape room set-ups are most effective when used with small groups. The presenter can stand in the middle and the participants can all see each other which encourages participation and conversation. I haven't found it effective for large groups.

Turn Your Speaking Into Cash

Example:

Room and A/V Requirements:
How to Get the Most from Judi's Program

As Judi Moreo presents keynotes, seminars, and workshops, the room set up and logistics will vary depending on the program. We will forward those to you at the time of the booking. Judi is a professional and she wants to give your attendees the very best program possible. In order to insure that your participants get maximum benefit from her program, there are some things you can help us with:

1. Judi prefers to have a cordless lavaliere microphone so that she can move around when she speaks. If there is a head table or a lectern in the area where Judi is expected to speak, please set it back a few feet from the front of the stage, if possible, so Judi can walk in front of it.
2. Judi needs to see the faces of the members of the audience and they need to see her facial expressions, so please leave full house lights on during the program. On the programs where she uses a power point, please unscrew ceiling bulbs above the screen, if possible.
3. We will furnish you with an introduction. The introduction is written specifically for each program to let the audience know why this speaker is qualified to speak on this subject. Therefore, PLEASE read the introduction the way it is written or something relatively close. Please don't tell the audience that the introduction says to read it the way it is written.

Judi Moreo

4. Please don't have moments of silence or sad announcements before Judi speaks. While it is appropriate to do this, we ask you not to do it right before her program as it brings the audiences' energy level down and the program will not be as successful.
5. Please don't schedule Judi to speak after an extended cocktail party. After cocktails, most attendees don't want to hear any speaker, no matter how good they are.
6. If you are presenting awards or have extended announcements, please either schedule Judi before the awards or give the audience a quick break before introducing her.
7. If you are interested in taping Judi's program, please contact us in advance to make arrangements at (702) 283-4567. If photos are to be taken, please be sure it is after the first 15 minutes of the program as the photographer and the flash are distractions for the audience.
8. Judi will be available to you to meet members of your organization and attend your social events, if requested. Please don't keep her out late the night before her presentation. It is imperative that she get her beauty sleep if she is to be at her best for your audience.
9. If Judi is speaking at a meal function, please order her meal to include protein and green vegetables. Judi is hypoglycemic and doesn't eat starchy foods, yellow vegetables, fruits, or desserts. If your meal function is a buffet, she can make her own selections so no special order will be required.
10. If any of the doors to the room make a loud noise when they close, please have a monitor so the door doesn't slam and make a distraction.

Turn Your Speaking Into Cash

Thank you very much for helping us with these items. If any of these things cause you extra work, we can be flexible. Our concern is the benefit to and the enjoyment of the audience members. Ineffective room set up, lighting, and distractions can sabotage the best of programs!

Question 28

Should I Put My Contact Information on Hand Out Materials?

Participants like to have materials that have the major points of your presentation that they can take home and review. Be sure to include information about you and how to contact you (your address, phone number, website, email, and social media addresses.)

I usually put this information in small type in the footer of every page of the handout and on any power point slides which I may be using.

Question 29

What Kind of Evaluation Sheets Should I Use?

Many people use a numbers scale on their evaluation forms. I choose not to do that because a number doesn't tell me anything. What one person thinks a number represents is not at all what another person thinks. Instead I choose to ask three brief questions which will get me specific information as to what the audience member thought about the program. This helps me continue to improve my presentations.

Turn Your Speaking Into Cash

INTERNATIONAL

3315 E. Russell Road, A4-404, Las Vegas, NV. 89120

Evaluation

What I loved about the program was:

What I will take away from today's program and use in my life/business/career:

I think the program could have been better if:

Name_____

Email_____ Phone_____

I would like to receive Judi's newsletter/magazine. Yes ____ No ____

I am interested in more programs of this type. Yes ____ No ____

I am interested in group coaching. Yes ____ No ____

Judi Moreo – (702) 283-4567 judi@judimoreo.com

The information at the bottom of the evaluation gives me permission to keep in touch with them on a regular basis by mailing a newsletter and lets me know whether there is an opportunity to work with them further.

Question 30

Do I Need to Send Out A Newsletter?

Sending a regular newsletter to your clients, potential clients, bureaus and audience members builds trust. Once people have heard you speak, you have made an impression on them and usually, they will want to hear from you again.

Your newsletter should have articles with valuable content for your readers as well as information about you. In my newsletter, I include a letter from me, then an educational or motivational article, recommended reading tips, a quote of the month, some sort of a mind exercise for them to do, then three short testimonials from other clients, my contact information and social media links. Don't make the articles too long as people don't have a lot of time. Have them relatively short and very interesting. People like pictures, so be sure to include several...a great headshot and several action shots.

Be sure to brand the newsletter with your colors, slogan, and logo.

Turn Your Speaking Into Cash

Example Newsletter

Judi Moreo

Our latest issue of Choices Magazine is ready for reading on-line at www.choicesonlinemedia.com. There are great articles by Jim Cathcart, Lou Sowers, D'Arcy Burke, Selena Torres, Becky Davis, Gina Geldbach-Hall, Kevin B. Parsons, Charlotte Foust, Joan Peck, Alisa Weis, and of course, me. I had a wonderful interview with watercolor artist, Ed Klein, and we are featuring some of his beautiful paintings in this issue. This is the relationship issue, so I know it will be of interest. It's about all types of love affairs and relationships. And notice that our writers are coming to us from around the globe. It's exciting to be creating an international magazine. Back issues are available for reading as well in our archives. If you want to print out a copy, go ahead. Enjoy!

My schedule for the next few months is very busy. Africa for the month of February. In the month of March, I'm in Seattle and Portland presenting some Communication Workshops. On March 29th, I'll be at the Spring Fling Book Fair put on by the Clark County Library District in Las Vegas. April, I have programs in Lincoln and Omaha, Nebraska, Alamosa and Durango, Colorado, Farmingham, New Mexico and Albuquerque. Then in May, I'll be in Texas most of the month. If you should get any of those letters saying I'm desperate and need money, please ignore it. Last year when I went to London, someone hacked into my email and asked everyone to send money to me. I promise not to ever send you any of those letters. But I must say, I was impressed with how many people called me to tell me they were sending the money. I sure hope no one actually sent any.

We saw the new Le Reve show at the Wynn the other evening. It was absolutely awesome. If you haven't seen it, when you come to Vegas, make it a must see.

Please go to Choices for more this month.

Remember, you are more than enough,

Judi

In 2010, we launched the first Life Choices book of short stories. Since that time, we have published four books in the series. The authors in these books shared their stories of what is possible when you choose to pursue the passion of your heart.

We have had so many requests to hear more from our authors that we have decided to create Choices magazine which we will publish four times a year: Spring, Summer, Autumn, and Winter. This is the fourth issue. Please let us know what you think.

Download Your Free Winter Issue of Choices Magazine Today!

Listen to Judi's radio show "Choices" on Blog Talk Radio.

Subscribe to *Winning Solutions*:

Subscribe today and you'll learn how to create the life you've always dreamed of.

Subscribe Now

Unsubscribe

© 2005-2014 Judi Moreo. All rights reserved. Feel free to use text from *Winning Solutions* in whole or in part as long as you include complete attribution, including live web site and e-mail links. Please also do us the courtesy of notifying us of where the material will appear.

Privacy Policy: We do not share any information about any subscriber with anyone for any reason. Period.

Question 31

Do Speakers Still Use Business Cards, Thank You Notes, & Greeting Cards?

You really should carry business cards with you everywhere. And hand out a minimum of 25 cards a day. Make your business card a standard size so your information can be easily added to a data base. If your card is oversized or tiny, it will probably end up thrown away or lost as it doesn't fit in standard scanners or card files. You can have a digital card which you text or email to others.

The important thing to remember is to put your picture on everything. People remember faces longer than they do names.

With the cell phones we have today, we can take a picture of ourselves with the client and put it on the front of the thank you card or a picture of ourselves with snow and a Christmas tree for a Christmas card. It's so easy to do, you should probably send a card for every holiday to keep yourself in the forefront of your client's minds.

Question 32

Should I Put My Picture on My Promotional Materials?

Everything you use to promote you should have your picture on it...website, promotional materials, products, business cards, your email signature. How will people know who you are if you don't advertise? One of my all-time favorite speakers, Ira Hayes, advocated putting your photo on everything including the letters you write. He even had postage-type stamps made with his photo so he could stick them on all promotional materials, letters, and envelopes.

Question 33

Should I Work with a Speaker Bureau?

Yes, when you are ready. Most bureaus work on commission and are only interested in booking you when you have a dynamic program and are truly a professional speaker. Bureaus look for people who are experts in particular subjects or fields and who have the marketing tools to make it possible to sell you. Most likely, in the beginning of your speaking career, you will need to book yourself. If you can't book yourself, when you know what you do better than anyone else, what makes you think a bureau can book you?

Bureaus make their money by booking speakers and it is far easier and takes less time to book someone who is already well known than to book a beginner. They must work twice as hard to book someone new to the industry. And your fee is much lower than some of the superstar speakers, so therefore, the bureau makes less money. However, if you are unique enough and have a great demo tape and marketing materials, you may just get lucky and find someone to represent you.

When you work with bureaus, be sure you work WITH them. Take their business cards along. Make up one

Turn Your Speaking Into Cash

sheets with their contact information. Give them copies of your books to send to their clients. Refer any leads that you get from one of their bookings back to them. All spin-off business should go through the bureaus. They put an incredible amount of time, money, and resources into promoting a speaker and the commissions are not all that high when you consider the overhead they have to pay. Be a speaker of integrity and refer all spin off business to the bureau that brought you to the client's attention in the first place.

Bureaus charge a percentage of your fee for booking you. It could be anywhere from 10% to 30%. Whatever it is, don't complain about it. They tell you what it is before you ever sign with the bureau. If you don't want to pay the commission, then don't sign an agreement with them. Get your own work. If you do sign an agreement with them, then honor it and keep your mouth shut. You wouldn't have had the business in the first place if they hadn't booked you. Never bad mouth the people you work with or for! It makes you look bad.

There are times when I don't have the time to do timely follow-up with potential clients, especially when over 100 people hand me their cards after my presentation. So, I will give these leads to a bureau for follow-up, even if the bureau didn't make the initial booking. They will usually get right to the task of follow-up. They appreciate the referrals and the commission they earn. The people appreciate that someone got back to them right away and I appreciate that the attendees got called. This shows your bureau that you are truly working in partnership with them.

Question 34

Should I Send Gifts to Meeting Planners and Bureaus?

It is always appropriate to send a thank you when someone has done something for you. If a meeting planner or a speaker bureau has booked you, certainly send a thank you gift. It is also appropriate to send a small gift to the person who did your introduction.

Don't send gifts as bribes. They are not appreciated. Any time you send a gift before you speak to the group, it looks like a bribe. Send it after your presentation along with a hand-written thank you note about how much you appreciated all they did for you. Also, don't send items that have your company logo or name on them and consider them gifts. That is advertising, not a gift.

In addition, send thank you notes to all the people who were involved in putting on the event and making it happen...like the tech guys and the lady who helped at your product table. We never know who else they work with or when they will be able to recommend us. I can't tell you how many times I have gotten presentations because the Catering Manager at a major Las Vegas hotel heard me speak and started telling her clients about me. She's right at the top of my Christmas gift list.

Question 35

What Is A Speaker Showcase and Should I Do Them?

Showcases are often put on by a bureau to introduce the speakers they represent to their clients and potential clients. The speakers who are offered the opportunity to participate are listed with that bureau. The speakers have approximately 15 minutes on stage to present their best material and showcase their talent.

The meeting planners and association executives who are sitting in the audience will have been supplied a booklet with information about the speakers who are presenting. They will make notes in the booklet about the speakers they see and like or do not like. Sometimes they will book speakers for an engagement before they leave the showcase. Other times, they will take the booklet back to their offices, put it in a file until the next time they have a need for a speaker and will wait until then to make the booking. I have had clients call to book me two years after they saw me in a showcase.

Participating in a speaker showcase that is presented specifically for meeting planners and association executives is fabulous exposure. Speakers will usually pay a fee to participate in this type of showcase. That

Turn Your Speaking Into Cash

fee covers the expense of putting on the showcase and promoting it. The coordinators of these usually don't make money on the showcase. They make their money when you get bookings and they get a percentage of that booking. It's hard to tell at the time of the showcase whether your investment will pay off, but if you are a good speaker and have a subject of interest to corporate and association clients, presenting in showcases is usually worth the investments of both your time and money.

When a client speaks with you at the showcase and wants to know your fee or asks you to send them more information, immediately turn them over to the bureau representative who is at the showcase and let them speak to that person. It is their job to do the booking, not yours.

Question 36

How Do I Track My Business?

It is imperative that you have a system for keeping track of inquiries and bookings. Whether you prefer a paper system, or a technology system is up to you.

A good contact management system that many speakers use is ACT. You will be able to set up custom fields for information that you will need from prospects and clients such as the name of the organization, address, contact name/s, date and location of next meeting, when they will be planning for the event, how many speakers they use at their events, and what fees you quoted them.

Keeping track of your contacts allows you to follow up with existing and potential clients, makes it easier to file your tax return at the end of the year and gives you a marketing list to call when you are looking for bookings for the upcoming year.

Question 37

How Do I Get Information About the Groups Which Hire Me?

Most companies and associations have websites. Go there and review thoroughly before putting your program proposal together. Ask meeting planners to add you to their mailing lists to receive trade publications. Send the client a Pre-Program Questionnaire and ask him to fill in as much information as he feels is pertinent to your presentation and return to you.

Question 38

How Much Should I Invest in My Career?

As much as you can afford. Just remember, it is a lot less expensive to get into the speaking business than it is into almost any other business. All businesses need to let people know they are in business, so the first investments you need to make are:

- any training or coaching you need in order to become an unforgettable speaker
- a demo video (known as a sizzle reel)
- a website
- a one sheet
- specifically, targeted advertising/marketing campaigns
- a newsletter
- a dynamite wardrobe including shoes
- a personal maintenance crew*

*manicurist, hairstylist, make-up consultant, image consultant, personal trainer, dry cleaner

Question 39

Should I Hire Someone to Do Public Relations for Me or Should I Do It Myself?

If you can afford to hire a good public relations firm to promote you, do so. Most speakers don't have the resources at the beginning of their careers to pay for promotion. So, you need to understand that you are your own best pr. How you behave and treat others speaks loudly about who you are and is as important off stage as it is on.

Don't act like you think you are a celebrity. Be down to earth and be interested in others. Be yourself. Be your best self. Be authentic. Don't put on "airs" or pretend to be something you are not. Be on your best behavior always.

Learn table manners. Speakers very often sit at head tables during meals and eat with some very influential people. How you hold your utensils tells on you. I have seen some very well-known speakers with some unspeakable table manners. Don't make a fist around the neck of your utensils. Don't dip your bread in the community butter dish. Know on which side of your

Turn Your Speaking Into Cash

plate your bread dish and drink reside. If you know this, you won't be drinking out of someone else's glass.

The most astonishing bad example I have seen (next to the car dealer taking the blind man's food) was at a speaker luncheon. Everyone at the table was a professional speaker. I noticed the woman across from me was nonchalantly bending the tines on her fork as she was speaking to me. Then she reached over her shoulder with the fork, inserted it down the back of her dress, and used it as a backscratcher.

Be prompt in all business matters. Return phone calls, answer letters and emails promptly. Be on time for any in-person meetings. Don't have the meeting planner wonder where you are at the last minute before you are to go on stage. Be there an hour early to make sure everything is working correctly. Call the meeting planner the night before to assure her that you are on top of things and will be there on time for your presentation. Also, be sure the meeting planner has your cell number so she can contact you while you are traveling or at the last moment, if necessary.

I always call the meeting planner when I arrive and let her know that I am on property, so she doesn't wonder if I have arrived. If I am not exhausted from the trip, I often ask if I can help with anything. One meeting planner was so thrilled, she asked me to come down and help her write "Happy Day" notes to the attendees. She was going to slip them under their room doors once they had gone to bed. I helped her write and deliver them. I did a powerful speech for her audience the next day, but I honestly feel that the next five times she booked me were a direct result of helping her with a project that really needed to get done.

Be considerate of people's time. Keep your presentation within the time parameters given. Running over throws the schedule of the entire program out of whack. Running over and causing the audience to miss their break or the next speaker not to have time to set up his equipment or worse yet, running into the other speaker's time is inconsiderate and unprofessional. One speaker who was on before me ran over his time, through the break, and forty minutes into my time before the meeting planner asked him to quit. Then I only had 15 minutes left for my presentation before their lunch break and I didn't feel I gave my best performance.

The meeting planner did, however, have me back the next year to do my entire program, so I guess my preview from the year before was better than I had felt it was.

That once happened to Ira Hayes and the second year, when he opened his speech, he started with "As I was saying...." And it brought the house down with laughter, as everyone remembered what had happened to him the year before.

Listen to others. Take the time to really listen to what people say to you and always direct the conversation along constructive lines.

Give praise when it is deserved. Be sincere about it. Look for and find things to praise in others.

Be cheerful...even if you don't feel like it. Smiles are contagious.

Turn Your Speaking Into Cash

Use polite words. You'll build friends fast when you use words such as "please," "thank you," and "my pleasure." Avoid profanity or saying anything that would be offensive to anyone in the audience. (Yes, there are speakers who are offensive on stage and some of them even command audiences for a year or two, but they are not respected by the majority and their careers are usually not long term.)

Be enthusiastic. Look for the bright side of situations. Look for virtues in people, not faults.

Be courteous. Remember Tony Alessandra's Platinum Rule, "Do unto others as they would have you do unto them."

Keep informed   Stay up-to-date on information, technology, and current events.

Know what you are to accomplish for the organization with the presentation you are giving. Don't let your ego get so carried away with yourself that you think the program is all about you. No matter how famous you become, the program is still about the audience.

Perform to the very best of your ability – every time. Discipline yourself to do what must be done when it should be done. Be willing to grow by doing a bit more than is expected of you.

Go the "extra mile." If another speaker doesn't show, have a second program that you know how to do and offer to do it for the meeting planner at no additional charge or at a reduced rate. It never hurts to pull a meeting planner out of a pinch. It is important to create relationships with your clients.

Get to know your client and his organization's purpose, ideals, mission, principles, standards and clients. While you are on assignment for other organizations, you are a part of their teams. You should be doing everything possible to help them accomplish their goals.

Stay relevant. The world is changing rapidly. If you are a speaker who has been around a few years, it is important to update your material regularly. While some examples stay relevant for a long time, many do not. You don't want to come across as a "has been."

Follow through. Get your invoices to the bureau or client right away...for your presentation and your expenses. Send a thank you letter immediately.

Question 40

How Much Will I Make as A Paid Professional Speaker?

The sky is the limit. There are many ways to make money in the speaking business. You can make it through speaking fees, seminars, back-of-the-room product sales, product endorsements, sponsorships, webinars, podcasts, consulting fees, and coaching fees.

Some top speakers make as much as $800,000+ per year. Many business speakers get from $2,500.00 to $10,000.00 per speech. Keynote speakers can make anywhere between $1,500.00 and $25,000.00. Celebrity speakers can command a lot more. Even though celebrity speakers may not be as good at presenting as a professional speaker, their name recognition will draw people to the event.

A National Speakers Association survey indicated that 2.6% of members earn over a million dollars per year. There are also a lot of speakers who are not making a living. How much you make is up to you!

Speakers who are doing 120-175 dates a year don't have a well-balanced lifestyle. I don't care what they tell you. The travel alone is a killer! You can do about 50–60 paid engagements a year and still have a life. If your fees are conservatively $7,500.00 for a full day, $5,000.00 for a half-day and $2,500.00 for an hour speech, you will probably average out at about $4,000.00 per speaking date. That would bring in $200,000.00 to $240,000.00 per year. If you have product for back-of-the-room sales, and you use a system such as the one I use for promoting that product, you could very well double your income.

Very often when you are first starting out, you will do a few speeches at no fee to get experience and maybe to get your foot in the door. Being seen in person, if you are a good speaker, is the best advertising you can get. Be sure to always ask for a testimonial.

Even after you have been speaking a while, you will have many opportunities for no-fee speaking where you can sell product in the back-of-the room which could again increase your income considerably. When someone asks you to speak for their organization at no-fee, do your homework. How many people will they have in attendance? What are the buying habits of the attendees? Is there someone in the audience who can book you for a paid presentation? If the no-fee engagement is to raise money for a charity and you want to do it as a donation, by all means, do it and get a letter from the organization for a tax deduction. But remember, every time you speak for free, you are in direct competition with the you that gets paid to speak. Once the word gets out that you will speak for free, more people will call and ask you to do a free program.

If the company says they don't have it in the budget for a speaker, you might want to barter. Perhaps in their educational budget, they have money for books. If they

buy a large number of books from you, then you can give them a "complimentary" program or "waive your fee." Don't ever say that you will give them a "free speech."
If they own a salon or a spa, perhaps you can trade for services. One of my clients owns a couple of small boutique hotels in Africa. I trade my one-hour training program for a week's stay at each of their hotels which includes all meals, hotel suite, and a day at each of their spas for myself and another person. Not a bad exchange for an hour program at each of their properties. If you are just starting out, you may need testimonial letters or video of your presentation. You can barter for these.

Then there are the pay-to-play speaking engagements. People actually ask you to pay to be on their stage. The only time that makes any sense is if you are a vendor at the event and you can give such a dynamic speech people will rush over to your booth and buy whatever product you have to offer. And you want that item to be a high-ticket item such as coaching or registration for a seminar. Paying to give a speech in order to sell a $19.95 book doesn't make sense. Even if you sell ten of those books, it is still under $200.00 and you have to figure up what it cost you to participate as well as the cost of the books. You could end up at a loss rather than a profit.

Question 41

How Will I Get Paid?

It is important for you to have a fee schedule. Know what you are worth and set your fees. Give the client some options. You will probably have one price for your keynote and a slightly lesser fee for workshops and breakout sessions. You could offer them a keynote plus a breakout session as well. In addition, you will need to charge for your expenses.

Once you and the client have agreed that you will speak for their event and you have agreed on the fee, you will send the client an Agreement. In some cases, they will send the agreement to you, but most of the time, it is your responsibility to send it to them. This Agreement should spell out the terms you have agreed upon. I have included a copy of the Agreement I use. As you can see, it is very simple. Many speakers have much more complicated Agreements, but I have found this one to work and I've never had any problems.

I request a 50% deposit at the time the Agreement is signed and the balance to be paid on the day of the presentation. Some clients prefer to pay the entire amount up front. Travel expenses are usually billed following the presentation and are due within 30 days.

Turn Your Speaking Into Cash

Some clients want to know up front what the total amount is going to be including all expenses. In that case, I do some homework on the cost of airfare to their area, hotel rooms, car service or rental car, etc. Then I estimate the total amount and add that into the fee. I like doing it this way because then I can travel as I like to travel and don't have to account for each item to the client. Plus, when the trip is over, I am paid and there is no more money to collect.

Example Fee Schedule

(Your Logo Here)

Speaking Fee Schedule
Effective January 1, 2019
All rates quoted in U.S. Dollars

Local:
Keynote Presentations . . . .$ 7,500
Up to 3 Hours (1/2 Day) . . . .$ 8,000
Up to 6 Hours (Full Day) . . . .$ 10,000

National:
Keynote Presentations . . . .$ 10,000
Up to 3 Hours (1/2 Day) . . . .$ 11,000
Up to 6 Hours (Full Day) . . . .$ 12,500

International:
Keynote Presentations . . . .$ 15,000
Up to 3 Hours (1/2 Day) . . . .$ 16,000
Up to 6 Hours (Full Day) . . . .$ 17,500

Plus Expenses

YOUR INVESTMENT includes all research, planning, program design, and visual aids plus the creation of program training materials (as needed).

EXPENSES include airfare, ground transportation, hotel accommodation, meals, tips and any materials/workbooks/handouts.

A/V REQUIREMENTS: Lavaliere Microphone, LCD projector, screen.

The fee quoted is based on the fact that there will be no audio or video recordings made of the presentation. Permission for audio/video recordings must be made through (your company name) and usage fees may be negotiated.

Your Letterhead w/Logo & Address

SPEAKER AGREEMENT

Client Name & Title
Organization Name
Address
E-mail

Thank you for choosing (Your Company Name) for your presentation needs. Please take a moment and review the terms of agreement.

Client:	Client Name
Presentation Title:	Name of Topic or Presentation
Speaker:	Speaker Name, Company Name
	Tax ID: XX-XXXXXXX
Dates & Presentation Times:	Date
	Beginning Time – Ending Time
Event/Venue:	Address of Where Presentation will Take Place
Educational Materials:	Number of Workbooks or Handouts included.
Investment:	$xx,xxx.xx to include educational materials.
Payment Terms:	Fees can be paid in full in advance or 50% ($xxxx.xx) in advance to secure the dates and the balance of 50% ($xxxx.xx) at the time of presentation.
Travel Expenses:	Will be billed at completion of trip and will include airfare, hotel, ground transportation, airport parking, and meals
Payment Terms:	30 days

(Your company name) agrees to provide:
- A Professional Speaker
- Materials for attendees
- Certificates of attendance

Client agrees to provide:
- Meeting facility
- Audio/video equipment as specified
- Any food/refreshment to be served

Cancellation or Rescheduling: If (Client Name) cancels the presentation date, (Your Company Name) will retain 50% of the presentation fees to cover business costs incurred. If (Client Name) changes any scheduled training within 30 days of the scheduled training dates (Your Company Name) will invoice $750.00 to cover business costs incurred. Please note that changes to speaking topics or times could result in additional charges.

(Your Company Name) Materials: (Client Name) acknowledges that the presentation materials and content are the property of (Your Company Name) and that the copyright, interest in and title to the presentation materials and content and any trademarks or service marks relating thereto remain with (Your Company Name.) Neither (Client Name) nor its authorized users shall have the right, title, or interest in the presentation materials and content except as expressly set forth in this agreement. This document serves as a binding agreement between (Your Company Name) and (Client Name).

Video taping of this presentation is forbidden unless given permission in writing in advance by a corporate officer of (Your Company Name).

If any information in this confirmation is incorrect or needs to be changed, please make immediate contact with (Your name and number.)

We are looking forward to working with you to make this important presentation your best one ever.

Your Signature Below Indicates Acceptance of the Above Terms:

_____   _____
(Client Name)   Date

_____   _____
(Your Company Name)   Date

Please sign and return one copy to (Your Company Name).

Question 42

What Regular Expenses Will My Business Require?

You will, of course, have the expenses of your office (if you have one), website, social media advertising, telephone, utilities, equipment, office supplies, printing, postage and you may get to the point of needing a staff member or two to assist you. Your biggest expense will probably be in the area of marketing. And remember, you will need a business license and a sales tax license. If you incorporate, you will have attorney fees, officer filing fees, and most likely, accounting fees.

Keep track of your costs. Little things can add up. This is why I insist that you regard your speaking as a business. You should make it a point that your expenses not exceed 50% of your income. Your accountant will want this information in order to file your taxes, so keep track of your expenses daily. It is easier to record daily than it is to scramble for the information on April 14th.

You should also look for opportunities to increase your income without increasing your number of speaking engagements. There are two ways of doing this.

Turn Your Speaking Into Cash

1. You can increase your income per engagement. Remember, you can only increase your engagement fee if you are an outstanding speaker. How do you know when you are ready to increase your fee? That will be when you have all the speaking engagements you can possibly handle at your current fee.

2. You can increase your income by increasing your per capita sales. This means increasing the amount of money each attendee spends with you.

You do this by adding products and services (that don't take a large amount of your time) that clients want to spend their money to get. You can learn how to do this. Depending upon the demand for your topic, the products and services that you offer, and the value of your ideas to your audience so that they want to invest their money in your products and services, it is possible to make in excess of $500,000.00 per year from 50 engagements.

Question 43

Should I Have Products to Sell?

Many speakers have told me they aren't good at sales or they aren't in the book business. My usual question for them is, "If you aren't good at sales, how can you be a speaker?"

Speakers are salespeople. Every time we are on stage, we are selling our ideas to others. If we can't sell our ideas, we won't get many repeat performances.

Regarding not being in the book business, how much can you teach a person in an hour? How much will they remember from a half day seminar? If you have a book that has the information which they need in it, you are doing the audience an injustice not to offer it to them. If they don't have take-away materials from your presentation, what will they refer to? People need to have educational materials. We should be encouraging lifelong learning throughout every presentation.

In addition, you need product for credibility. When you have a published book, you are an instant expert. Your book becomes one of your best promotional tools. When you are seeking business from a client, send your book with a letter of introduction. Instant credibility. If you are competing against another speaker for an engagement,

Turn Your Speaking Into Cash

you send your book and they don't have one to send, who do you think gets the engagement? Usually the person with a book. If you also send along your CD or your DVD, the meeting planner can listen to you while driving or watch your presentation at his leisure. If he hears or sees something that he really likes, you will probably be the one to get hired.

The packaging of your products should represent your brand and convey a message of success, knowledge, and excitement. Are your marketing efforts consistently high quality?

You should also package yourself with as much care. After all, you are your #1 product. When you show up, how do you look? Do you dress, sit, stand and present yourself as a successful businessperson? Are you well-groomed? Do you behave in a manner that says you are what you say you are?

My business partner and I were doing a public seminar with several other speakers in several cities. On the first morning of programs, all the speakers were downstairs early, setting up product for sale. When it was almost time for the program to start at about a quarter to eight, I turned to the lady who was doing the opening keynote and said, "Oh goodness, look at the time, You had better hurry, you only have 15 minutes to change." She looked like I slapped her and said, "This is what I'm wearing all day." I was so embarrassed. I had no idea that she actually spoke in clothing that looked like she might be going fishing. We sometimes wore this type of clothing to set-up product tables, check equipment and eat an early breakfast, and then rushed back to our hotel rooms to change into professional attire for our presentations so that is why I assumed she was going to change.

It is important to remember you are ALWAYS promoting yourself and therefore, your business. Even on the plane to your next engagement, remember the person next to you may be on his way to the same conference to hear you speak, or may even be someone in need of a speaker for his next conference.

Your attitude, how you speak to and treat people is as important as your attire and grooming. Be aware of your manners in the hotel restaurant, attendees may also be having a quick breakfast before the conference.

As you are your main product, presenting yourself with confidence and authority is not always easy. It helps to remember to use positive self-talk and always present yourself at your best.

Question 44

How Do I Get Product to Sell?

There are several ways to get product. You can buy other people's product for resale. You can make your own. You can write a book, or you can hire a ghost writer. You can RECORD EVERY PROGRAM YOU EVER DO. You can edit that recording and make a CD of it. You can even record your program, duplicate it without editing and sell it as a "live" program. You can transcribe it and have a manual. You can have a teleconference and record it. You can be a contributing author to an anthology. You can video your programs and make DVD's. You can buy your own CD and DVD duplicator and make the number that you think you will sell at each presentation or make new demos to send out whenever you feel the need. You can also:

- Turn your program into an on-line "course".
- Create a blog on your website with an archive and sell a subscription to archived material.
- Create short, informational e-books about different aspects of your topic.
- Co-author with another speaker
- Do a podcast, record it, and sell it as a product

I often trade books with other speakers who write in my genre. For instance: Jesse Ferrell writes self-help books like mine, so I like having a few of his books for sale on

Turn Your Speaking Into Cash

my product table. This tells my audience I am not only selling my books; I am bringing them quality products with valuable information for them.

Question 45

Why Would Someone Buy My Products?

Give people a reason to buy your product. Tell them that you've covered a lot, that you know they've taken extensive notes; then ask, *"but honestly, how often do you go home from a program and review your notes?"* Remind them that with your product, they can hear the information repeatedly. Repetition is the key to learning and in addition, you didn't have time to share with them all that you know. There is so much more information they need that is in the product. If you DON'T do this, people won't know why you have product or why they should buy it.

Give people instructions on how to buy your product. Say something along the lines of *"Take out your order form and let's fill it out together. (Help them by recommending what to buy.) Get up, go to the back of the room, give your order to the person who is assisting (say name) and start your future TODAY."*

Or, at the beginning of the program you can say, *"I have left a product list in your chair. Fill out the top with your name and address now to save you time at the end of the day. As we go through the day, I will be recommending*

Turn Your Speaking Into Cash

resources to you, mark which learning resources will help you continue the learning from today. At lunch time (or break) take the form to the back of the room. Give it to the program assistant along with your payment information and she will have your product ready for you to pick up when you are ready to leave today."

If you don't tell people exactly what it is you want them to do, they won't do anything.

Question 46

What Should I Know About Seminar Companies?

Working for a seminar company is a very good way to break into the speaking business. There are two major seminar companies to which you can apply: Fred Pryor Seminars and SkillPath. They are both located in the Kansas City area. I have worked for both as well as National Seminars Group.

To apply, you must send a video tape. It doesn't have to be a professional video, but you should appear professional. Once they have seen your tape and like what they see, you will be asked to go to Kansas City for an interview. Sometimes, you can do the interview on-line. Be prepared to do a live presentation for the interview. In some cases, they will have their entire sales staff in the room to observe you and then they discuss if they can sell you or not.

If they hire you, you will need to attend their certification class. This usually takes two days and you will pay your own expenses to get to their office and for your hotel. There is a charge for the certification class. You can negotiate how you pay for this. In many cases, you pay

Turn Your Speaking Into Cash

half the fee upfront and they will take the balance out of your pay once you are officially hired and working.

When you work with a seminar company, you learn their programs and present them to their audiences. They pay you a daily rate plus a per diem for your expenses. They book your travel, rental cars, and hotels and usually pay for those in advance. You will need a credit card to check into hotels and to charge any expenses you incur at the hotel.

The seminar company offers you a certain number of days work each month. Once you agree to the dates, you are expected to fulfill them. They will book you a week at a time, for four or five cities per week, Sometimes, you will be on a program with other speakers and will travel with them. Other times you will present the entire program and travel by yourself. When traveling with the other speakers, try to get along with them and don't badmouth the company. Keep your negative personal opinions to yourself, even if they don't.

You will be expected to sell products...books, tapes, other seminars and yearly seminar memberships. This can be valuable experience for you. When you get good at sales, you can increase your daily income through commissions. The more you sell, the more money you make. And, down the road, when you have your own product to sell, you will already know the most effective way to do it.

Get to know the products you are selling. Read the books. View the videos. The more you know about them, the easier it will be to tell participants about the value to them from owning these products. Doing this will help you deliver the program with more confidence and in turn increase your product sales. And, you get a great education by reading and viewing all these products.

Learn to pack light, You want everything you take with you to fit into one carry-on bag, You don't want to have to wait for luggage to arrive when you arrive at your destination and you sure don't want to have to lug around several suitcases all week. One poor speaker I traveled with brought three suitcases and a wardrobe bag in addition to her carry-on. Needless, to say she learned during that first week what a burden all that stuff can be when you need to travel fast and/or you are traveling with other speakers.

Whether you are a man or a woman, you need to own three professional sets of clothing. Two to take with you and one in the dry cleaners. Be sure to make friends with your dry cleaners as you will be dropping off and picking up on Saturdays.

You will be in a different city every day, so you can wear the same clothing more than once. If you own a great suit, you can probably wear it all week and change your blouse or shirt each day.

You also need to wear comfortable shoes, for standing all day and for running through airports. I took gym clothes that could double for pajamas and wore my gym shoes on the plane.

You will appreciate me telling you to cut down on the wardrobe when you realize that in that carry-on you must also carry your own equipment...computer, projector,

Turn Your Speaking Into Cash

microphone, extension cord, and power strip. There just isn't room for a half dozen pairs of shoes.

Don't expect them to put you in the Ritz-Carlton. You will often be staying in inexpensive hotels and motels. Some of them will not have elevators and you will have to carry your luggage up and down steps. Many of these places don't have restaurants so carry nutritional snacks with you.

On the day of your seminar, you will need to go downstairs about 6 or 6:30 am to be sure the room is set-up correctly, set up your own equipment and make sure it is working, set up the product display table and meet the program coordinator. You may have to help the program coordinator stuff the attendee packets with workbook, evaluation forms, and product order forms. If you don't have a coordinator for some reason, you will have to stuff these packets yourself and you will need to be at the registration table by 8 am to welcome and register the guests.

On your breaks, you will be selling product and at the end of the day, you will pack up any left over product to ship back to the company, tally up all sales, and put in a Federal Express envelope along with credit card charge slips, any money that you collected, and the evaluation forms and drop into the nearest Federal Express box. Be sure you drop it in the box. Don't give it to hotel employees to do for you. You are responsible for the money in that envelope. Be sure you make a note in your file of how many attendees you had, how much money was collected and the location of the box where you dropped it. You will need this information to keep track of commissions due you and also to track the envelope in case the company doesn't receive it in a timely manner.

Then you drive to the next city and do it all over again the next day.

Being a "road warrior" is not easy. You must be in good physical health. You will need stamina and patience. If something can go wrong, it usually will. By now, you are probably asking yourself why anyone would do this. Some speakers do it because they love working with people and sharing information with people who want to learn, some like the potential of making very good money, and others are in it to get the experience of speaking to a different audience day after day. If you work for a seminar company for a year, you will become a very good speaker. You will encounter experiences you never would have imagined. And, you will learn a lot about yourself.

Seminar Companies

Fred Pryor Seminars
P. O. Box 219468
Kansas City, Missouri 64121-9468
www.pryor.com
1-800-780-8476
speakerapp@pryor.com

SkillPath
6900 Squibb Rd
Mission, Kansas 66202

SkillPath Canada
45 Zimmerman St. South
#d-2
Strathroy, Ontario N76 0a3
www.skillpath.com
1-800-873-7545

Both companies have a place to apply on-line.

Question 47

What About Presenting Seminars on My Own?

Speakers who promote and conduct their own seminars can earn twenty to thirty times as much in a day as they can conducting some other company's seminars. Of course, there is the marketing aspect. You must market the seminar to get people to attend.

Some of the things to remember in promoting your own seminar are:

1. Select a topic that will sell
2. Understand what result you want from the seminar
3. Market, market, market
4. Customers usually don't buy from a one-time contact
5. Customers need lots of information
6. Aggressive follow-up is needed

You will also need to understand the logistics involved in the actual presentation of the seminar. Besides promoting, you must also be available or have online capability of accepting reservations and payment. Tracking the number of registered participants is a critical aspect of your success.

Turn Your Speaking Into Cash

Secure an appropriate location. If you don't have a built-in meeting room in your office, you must make arrangements at a hotel, convention space, office complex or other environment that has easy access, ample parking and the capability of providing catering or lunch services, if you are doing an all-day program.

Before you begin marketing your seminar, you must have an idea of the expenses you will incur in presenting the program. What will the marketing cost? Will you provide workbooks or handouts? If so, will you print them yourself or have them done professionally? Don't forget to include the cost of your paper and toner if you print your materials yourself. Will you provide refreshments such as bottled water and mints on the tables or a full luncheon? Will you provide note pads and pens, or will the facility provide those for you?

If you are working with a hotel or convention services location, be sure to get details of all costs including room rental, food and beverage, audio/visual, set up charges, staffing charges, local taxes and fees. You will need to take these things into consideration when you are setting a fee for your program.

You will also need to be able to take credit cards and have a way for people to pay for registration and your products on-line or over the phone. There are several systems available, PayPal & Square are the most commonly used and, I find them to be user friendly. Your back of the room sales will increase if you can take credit cards. In addition, it is easier to close most any sale if you have the ability for someone to charge.

Question 48

How Do I Get Names of People Who Might Want to Attend My Seminars, Hire Me to Do A Speech, Or Buy My Products?

This is what is meant by "building a database" or "your list." You can do this in several ways. The most important being to ask for the information.

When you are speaking somewhere or exhibiting, pass around a clip board or iPad and have people sign up to receive your newsletter, a free booklet, or gift of some kind. Usually best to offer something in addition to or instead of a newsletter. How many more newsletters do you want to receive in your inbox?

I tell people I am going to put them on my mailing list, and they will have the opportunity to opt in. By giving me permission to be on my list, they receive a complimentary subscription to *Choices Magazine*, a positive mental attitude magazine which I publish four times a year. You can get the magazine as well, if you go to my website www.judimoreo.com and sign up.

Turn Your Speaking Into Cash

You can put a place on your program evaluation form that asks the participant to give you the name, phone number and email address of someone who might enjoy hearing a program such as the one they have just attended.

Tom Winninger is a master at getting repeat and spin off business by simply saying something along the lines of, *"As you can see, I am very passionate about today's material. If you know of a company or association who might benefit from a presentation such as this, please come up after the program and hand me your business card."*

Many speakers send out a monthly electronic newsletter free of charge. If you have a newsletter, mention it during your presentations and say, *"If you would like to receive my newsletter at no cost to you, just give me your business card before you leave today or sign up on the clipboard at the product table."*

At public seminars, you can do a drawing for a product. People can drop their business cards into a box for the drawing. It's a good idea to have some small pieces of pre-printed paper for people to fill out and drop in the box, if they don't have a business card. Be sure to have pens and/or pencils there as well.

If you are doing a power point presentation, be sure that your website appears on all slides. Also include your website on all handout materials and giveaway items.

With any of these techniques, it is a good idea to clear it with the meeting planner ahead of time.

When you get home, be sure to follow up with those people who gave you their information. You want to be sure to let them know right away that you appreciate their participation. Don't wait too long or they may just forget who you are!

Question 49

Should I Join A Speakers' Organization?

One of the best ways to learn and understand any business is to not only join but to actively PARTCIPATE in the industry professional organization. These organizations provide both educational and networking opportunities. In the speaking profession, organizations often have members who are also bureau owners, meeting planners and other people who can benefit your career.

Speaking organizations that are beneficial to you:

Toastmasters International
9127 S. Jamaica Street, Suite 400
Englewood, Co. 80112
+1 (720) 439-5050   Fax +1 (303) 799-7753
www.toastmastersinternational.org

A world leader in helping people become more competent and comfortable in front of an audience. This nonprofit organization now has nearly 226,000 members in 11,500 clubs in 92 countries, offering a proven – and enjoyable! – way to practice and hone communication and leadership skills.

Turn Your Speaking Into Cash

NSA - National Speakers Association
1500 South Priest Drive
Tempe, Arizona 85281
480-968-2552
www.nsaspeaker.org

The leading professional association for speakers, providing resources and education designed to advance the skills, integrity and value of its members and the speaking profession. Most major cities have a local NSA chapter.

GSF - The Global Speakers Federation
www.globalspeakersfederation.net

The Global Speakers Federation champions, supports and provides resources to help develop and grow associations of professional speakers worldwide.

GSF aims to:
1. Strengthen worldwide recognition of professional speaking within the meetings industry.
2. Provide support to member associations on forming, managing, and leading associations, including sharing best practices.
3. Build a global community of like-minded people to encourage alliances, connections, and support networks.

The GSF currently comprises 15 independent speaker associations representing 17 nations and individuals from over 20 countries.

Question 50

Are There Other Professional Organizations to Which I Should Belong?

You should be aware of the following organizations as most of our clients will belong to one or more of these. These are organizations whose members can hire speakers for their conferences and conventions. How well you can connect with the members of these organizations will determine your success or failure as a speaker in the association market. The members of these groups have meetings and associations of their own. They usually have a national convention once a year, but they also have lots of other meetings. Speak at their conventions, even if you do it complimentarily and pay your own expenses to get there. This is the best exposure you can possibly get, and you can't buy it. This is word-of-mouth on a jet ski.

Turn Your Speaking Into Cash

GCG Event Partners
125 Main Street, Suite H
Stoneham, MA 02180-1600
+1-866-GCG-Events (424-3836); +1-781-279-9887
www.gcgeventpartners.com

A network of over 1000 independent event planning industry professionals spanning the United States. Members have at least 3 years' experience and an average of 11 years' experience as professionals in the meetings and events industry. They are Meeting Planners, Travel Directors, Event Planners, and other professionals that have a wide array of qualifications, skills and experience.

ASAE - American Society of Association Executives
1575 I Street NW, Washington, DC
+1-888-950-2723; +1-202-371-0940;
Fax +1-202-371-8315
www.asaecenter.org

Known as the association of associations, ASAE is considered the advocate for the nonprofit sector. The society is dedicated to advancing the value of voluntary associations to society and supporting the professionalism of the individuals who lead them. Founded in 1920 as the American Trade Association Executives, with 67 charter members, ASAE now has 25,000 individual members who manage leading trade, professional, and philanthropic associations.

PCMA - Professional Conference Managers Association
35 E. Wacker Drive, Suite 500
Chicago, Illinois 60601
+1 (312) 423-7262
www.pcma.org

A nonprofit international association of professionals in the meetings industry whose mission is to deliver breakthrough education and promote the value of professional convention management.

ESPA - Event Services Professional Association
191 Clarksville Road
Princeton Junction, NJ 08550
P: 609.799.3712   F: 609.799.7032
espaonline.org

Founded in 1988, ESPA's mission is to provide the necessary education and preparation for members to excel within the events industry, and to play an important role in its innovation. Although the association initially served convention managers, ESPA has grown to include a diverse range of association members, from Catering Managers to Audio Visual technicians.

ESPA provides knowledge forums and continuing education hours to help members keep up with industry trends.

Turn Your Speaking Into Cash

NACE - National Association for Catering and Events
10440 Little Patuxent Parkway, Suite 300
Columbia, Md. 21044
+1-410-290-5410
www.nace.net

NACE is a national industry association with over 40 local chapters across the nation. Joining your local NACE chapter and attending their events is a great way to get involved in the larger organization. And it also offers the chance to network within your local market and meet your neighboring peers.

For those who want to explore NACE on a larger scale, check out the annual NACE Experience Conference. It's an incredible chance to take in both innovative education and plenty of networking opportunities with peers.

ACCED-I - Association of Collegiate Conference and Events Directors – International
2900 South College Ave., Suite 3B,
Fort Collins CO 80525
(970) 449-4960
www.acced-i.org

ACCED-I membership includes over 1,300 campus professionals who design, market, coordinate and plan conferences and special events on the campuses of colleges and universities around the world. ACCED-I has increased the visibility of the collegiate conference and events profession and hosts an annual conference to bring these planners together.

International Live Events Association
330 N. Wabash Ave, Suite 2000
Chicago, Il. 60611
+1-800-688-4737; +1-312-321-6853
www.ileahub.com

Besides networking with professionals from the industry and offering business opportunities, ILEA's (formerly ISES) focus is on providing a community by which event planners can build relationships and work together to discover ways to creatively develop the events industry. The community is really what drives this event planning association's success: ILEA has 53 chapters and over 5,500 members internationally. Membership ranges from meeting planners, caterers and decorators to journalists, audio-visual technicians and photographers.

MPI - Meeting Professionals International
27111 Lyndon B Johnson Freeway, Suite 600
Dallas, Texas 75234
+1 (866) 318-2743 Fax: +1 (972) 702-3065
www.mpiweb.org

Established in 1972, Dallas-based Meeting Professionals International (MPI) is the largest association for the meetings profession with more than 19,000 members in 80 chapters and clubs across the USA, Canada, Europe and other countries throughout the world.

Turn Your Speaking Into Cash

Corporate Event Marketing Association
916-740-3623
www.cemaonline.com

CEMA is targeted specifically toward event marketing professionals. CEMA serves as a "thought leadership association" in that it fosters a community of event marketing professionals that share their expertise and experiences in order to further advance industry best practices. It also publishes white papers and maintains a blog in order to create relevant content for event marketing professionals.

International Congress and Convention Association
ICCA North America Office
Box 6833, Freehold, 07728-6833 New Jersey, U.S.A.
+1 732 8516603; Fax +1 732 8516584
www.iccaworld.org

ICCA is strongly dedicated to the future of the international events industry and offers membership as a means of providing event planning professionals with the opportunity to express their commitment to the craft of event organizing. ICCA is especially strong on the international front in its representation of meetings and events professionals across the world, offering professionals access to a truly international community. ICCA members can take advantage of a plethora of educational programs led by industry professionals, from expert seminars to forums for young professionals. ICCA is geared towards event organizers who do business internationally, because membership provides organizers with global networking events and to over 1,000 suppliers in the international meetings industry.

Judi Moreo

IAVM - International Association of Venue Managers
635 Fritz Drive, Suite 100
Coppell, TX 75019-4442 USA
+1 800.935.4226 or +1 972.906.7441 | Fax: +1 972.906.7418
www.iavm.org

IAVM provides event venue managers with educational resources and networking opportunities. IAVM particularly prides itself on being committed to the values of integrity, diversity, education, and service. IAVM members come from a diverse range of venue types. For example, active members include executives and managers from convention centers, university complexes, performing arts centers, and amphitheaters.

Eventovation
Eventovation.org

Launched in 2016, Eventovation is the fastest growing community for people in the event planning world. With nearly 800 members, Eventovation is an online forum and live networking series that facilitates learning and networking between event experts.

Members who belong to Eventovation range from corporate event planners for companies like Hewlett Packard, to freelance organizers, and event technology experts.

NCBMP - National Coalition of Black Meeting Planners
1800 Diagonal Road
Alexandria, VA 22314
571.366.1779
info@ncbmp.org

Founded in 1983, NCBMP is geared toward the training of African American meeting planners and is committed to improving the meetings and conferences industry. NCBMP's mission is to educate planners within the African American community on all facets of the planning profession and to provide a networking community that promotes professionalism and planning best practices.

SGMP - Society of Government Meeting Professionals
3337 Duke Street
Alexandria, VA 22314
+1-703-549-0892; +1-703-549-0708
www.sgmp.org

A nonprofit professional organization of persons involved in planning government meetings, either on a full or part-time basis, and those individuals who supply services to government planners.

Question 51

Should I Have A Personal Coach?

Whether you are a beginning speaker or a professional, a coach or a mentor can be very beneficial to you. Coaching is a process, not something you can do for one session, take a test and be a pro. Coaches don't tell us what to do or how to do it. They give us suggestions and guide us. They provide alternatives for us. And most of all, there is an element of accountability. Are you on track with your goals? What's missing? What's needed? What's next?

Any investment you make in your self-improvement is an investment forever. If you want to be a doctor, you go to medical school, spend a good deal of time and money and then intern for a number of years before starting your own practice. In speaking, you can start your business while being coached. You don't have to wait four or more years to begin.

In working with me as your personal coach, these are the areas of focus that you would explore over the course of a year:
- Evaluation of current presentation style and promotional materials
- Assistance in presentation development

Turn Your Speaking Into Cash

- Review of current presentations with suggestions and rewrite consultation
- Designing of promotional materials and developing your marketing tool kit
- Marketing guidance - learn to position yourself apart from the crowd and promote yourself effectively
- Manage your image
- Learn to set and negotiate fees
- Writing effective proposals
- Developing product offerings
- Structuring your back-of-the-room offer
- Positioning and setting up your product table
- Subliminal selling techniques
- Setting up your speaker office
- Form letters, organizational tools, and other methods to get your office running smoothly
- Effective telephone procedures including following up leads by telephone
- Techniques for how to get referrals, sign up multiple programs for one client, and create passive income
- Assistance in developing your newsletter to get bookings and sell products
- Rehearse all aspects of the delivery, offering strategic performance techniques
- Two-day "Turn Your Speaking into Cash" bootcamp held in Las Vegas, NV

If you are interested in my coaching services, contact me at judimoreo@yahoo.com or (702) 283-4567.

Question 52

Do I Have What It Takes?

You can be an unforgettable speaker if you believe you can. If you have an area of expertise, a personal story, information or knowledge people want and need, you can be successful as a paid, professional speaker.

Make your presentation unique and exciting. Practice until you know your material so well that it sounds as if you are having a conversation with the people in the audience. Speak to any and every group that you can. Boldly present your material. Give your best every time you present... whether to one person or 10,000.

Form a mental picture of your success. Begin developing and living your presentation mentally. Set goals for yourself. How many presentations do you want to give this year? This month? This week? How many do you want to book for next year? How many calls will you make each day?

Make a vision board and put it up in your office above your computer where you see it constantly. Put a picture of you speaking in the middle of the board, and around it, put the logos of all the companies and organizations for whom you want to speak.

Turn Your Speaking Into Cash

I put the logo of Stations Casinos on my vision board and it wasn't a week later when their HR Director called me to meet with her about writing curriculum for their training department. She was so surprised when I told her I had added their company logo to my vision board the week before, she asked to see it. I, of course, proudly showed it to her and got a nice contract.

Don't forget what I said about everybody in this business knowing everybody else. This is a relationship industry. So, start building relationships with bureaus, meeting planners and other speakers. Build relationships with your clients. Always be professional and behave in a manner that makes people proud to be associated with you. People do business with people they know and like. Meeting and event planners do business with people who make them look good. Make sure they can trust you to do that.

It's important to make friends. It is so exciting when you unexpectedly run into another speaker you know in an airport and you have a meal together or you trade seats with a passenger on the plane so you can sit next to each other for a couple of hours. This is not a business of competition. We are all in this together. We very often get work because another speaker recommended us. If someone calls and asks you to speak on a subject which you know nothing about, recommend a speaker who speaks about that subject. Some speakers pay a referral fee when they get an engagement for which you recommended them.

Some speakers who recommend you will ask you for a referral fee. I would never ask, but would always appreciate if you offer it. I have referred people to speak and never even received a thank you note. Don't let that be you. You be a professional, pick up the phone, call the other speaker and let them know if you got the engagement or not. Thank them. And offer them a referral fee. If they don't accept it, send them a small gift of something personal you know they will like.

This can be a very lonely business when you are out on the road week after week. You will spend a lot of time by yourself...in airports, hotels, driving in rental cars, and eating meals. More so in the USA than when we travel abroad. People in my audiences in other countries have always asked me to lunch and dinner, taken me to the opera and concerts, and checked with me to be sure I had everything I needed. The bureaus in those countries show a lot more personalized attention to someone from another country. They understand we are in unfamiliar territory and often they assign someone to travel with us and take care of our needs.

Perhaps the bureaus here do that for speakers from other countries.

When I was in Dubai, the client assigned two ladies the responsibility of taking me on tours and out to all my meals... for a week even though I only spoke for 45 minutes on one day.

When I was ill in England, my client hired a nurse to stay with me at the hotel for several days.

When I was in South Africa, I was treated like a superstar. I've been privileged to work with several bureaus in this country and they've all taken me into their homes and their lives and treated me like family.

Turn Your Speaking Into Cash

As I have now traveled to 29 countries, I could fill a book with wonderful stories about the people who have come into my life and become my friends. Perhaps I will write it soon.

In the meantime, I hope you will persist and persevere knowing that every audience with whom you speak, every client who hires you, every bureau who represents you and every speaker with whom you work is an important part of your life. Cease obsessing about "what people think about you" and dare to concentrate on what you can give to them. This will ensure that "what they think about you" is positive.

And remember, you are more than enough.

Judi

If you have found the information in this book to be helpful to you, will you please write me a brief testimonial letter telling me what results you have had and send to me at judimoreo@yahoo.com.

Or, if it's easier for you, just make a quick video testimonial on your phone and text it to me at (702) 283-4567.

I will greatly appreciate it.

Appendix

Glossary

Agent: A person who represents a speaker or speakers on an exclusive basis. They receive a percentage of everything the speaker makes. They sometimes handle publicity and promotion for the speaker as well.

Agreement: A contract between the speaker and client; the speaker and bureau; or the bureau and client.

Anthology: a collection of literary works chosen by the compiler. usually written by various authors. It may be a collection of poems, short stories, or plays.

Back of Room Sales (BOR): Product sales that are made from the back of the room when a speaker does a presentation. i.e. books, DVDs, CDs.

Bio: A biography of the speaker. It will be a synopsis of the speaker's career and major accomplishments such as book titles, television appearances, education and awards.

Booking: A confirmed speaking engagement.

Turn Your Speaking Into Cash

Break Out Session: A convention presentation that the attendees make a choice about attending. Usually there are several going on at one time which focus on different topics.

Bureau: A company that obtains bookings for speakers on a commission basis.

Byline: The line which appears on an article, story, book, play, or movie that acknowledges the authorship.

Client: The person, company, or organization that pays for the speaker to make a presentation.

Coach: A professional who teaches others how to succeed and encourages them to do so. Usually they receive a fee for their services.

Conclusion: Final remarks in a presentation.

Concurrent Sessions: Presentations that are happening at the same time as other presentations and attendees have a choice about which one to attend.

Consultant: A professional person who gives advice for which he charges a fee.

Contract: A written document used to spell out the agreement between two parties such as a speaker and client; or speaker and bureau.

Date: A definite booking.

Demo: A demonstration of the speaker's ability on audio or video. Used to promote the speaker to clients.

Emcee: The master or mistress of ceremonies. A person that is on stage and facilitates the agenda of a program.

Engagement: A booking or a date where the speaker has been employed to speak.

Exclusive: When the speaker has an arrangement with an agent, a manager, or a bureau to handle all his/her business.

Expenses: Business costs incurred by a speaker on behalf of the client or the clients' presentation i.e. airfare, rental car, hotel, meals, presentation and handout materials.

Fee: The amount the speaker is paid per each engagement.

General Assembly: A presentation that all attendees of a convention attend at one time. Not usually a meal function.

Gig: An entertainment term for a booking or engagement.

Gross: The total fee the client is charged for a speaker and presentation. This would include any agent or bureau fees but not expenses.

Handouts: Materials given out at a presentation to supplement the speaker's presentation.

Honorarium: A small token payment sometimes given to speakers when they are doing a program for no-fee.

Turn Your Speaking Into Cash

In House: A program done for one company's employees at their company location.

Introduction: An introducer speaks or reads information about the presenter to the audience immediately preceding the presentation. It is usually prepared by the speaker or the speaker's manager/agent and sent to the client ahead of time for familiarization. It should explain "Why this speaker for this audience."

Keynote: One of the main or featured speeches at an event. These presentations are used for opening or closing an event as well as at meal times.

Lavaliere: A microphone that is attached to a cord and hangs around the neck or has a clip to attach to your lapel, belt, or another part of your clothing so you do not need to hold it.

Lectern: A small stand that holds notes.

Manager: A person who handles the business affairs of a speaker.

Meeting Planner: A person in charge of planning and handling all logistics of a meeting.

On-Site: A program done at the location of the client.

PA: A public address system.

Panel: A group of people who discuss a subject in front of an audience. Often, the audience members can participate by questioning the panel.

Podium: A small stage or set of risers on which a speaker stands.

PR: Public relations.

Products: Books, CD's, DVD's that complement the speaker's topic and are available for purchase by attendees of the program.

Profit: The money left over after everyone else gets theirs. One of the main reasons you do all the work necessary to build a professional speaking career.

Projector: A piece of equipment used to project a picture onto a screen.

Property: The hotel or venue where the program is being presented.

Public Seminar: A seminar that is open to the public for which one may or may not have to pay to attend.

Q & A: A question and answer session that sometimes follows a presentation.

Risers: Portable platforms used to raise the height of the front of the room so that the presenters can be better seen by the audience.

Road Warrior: A person who's occupation keeps them traveling away from home.

Seminar: An educational session. Usually a classroom type lecture format with workbook or handouts.

Turn Your Speaking Into Cash

Testimonial: A recommendation by someone who is familiar with your work.

Tentative Hold: A date the speaker holds for a client and does not sell to anyone else until the client either makes a firm commitment or releases the date.

Trainer: A speaker who presents workshops on a subject or does training of employees for a client.

Venue: The meeting place. This can be a hotel, conference center, university, restaurant, or meeting room.

Workshop: An educational, classroom type session in which attendees can participate in the discussion and/or projects.

Life Affirming Resources by Judi Moreo

Judi Moreo is an internationally acclaimed speaker, author, and coach. For over forty years, Judi has studied the lives and habits of highly motivated and successful people. She has unraveled the mystery behind the illusion that only a chosen few are allowed success and has become a respected authority on high level performance, personal development, and self-esteem.

Her unique approach to helping people succeed has made her one of the most sought-after keynote speakers in the nation. You can now take advantage of her knowledge and expertise through her books.

You may order the following books online at: www.judimoreo.com/shop

You Are More Than Enough: Every Woman's Guide to Purpose, Passion & Power
This is a powerful guide to discovering your purpose, unleashing your passion, and changing your habits to realize the success you want in all the areas of your life ---personal and professional relationships, career, finances, and security.

The Achievement Journal
This is a life changing tool. It is a method for organizing goals, dreams, and expectations -- as well as evaluating what's working, what's missing, and what's needed to bring positive results into your life.

Turn Your Speaking Into Cash

Fast Track to Writing and Launching Your Book
Writing and publishing a book can give you huge exposure and help you establish expertise and authority in your market when done right. Planning is the key and that's exactly what this book will help you do every step of the way. When you have a plan in place for how you'll write, publish and market your book, the process is much more enjoyable and achievable.

Overcoming Cancer: A Journey of Faith
Through her personal story, inspiring quotes and practical suggestions, Judi shows us that cancer and fear are messages to us to make lifestyle changes. This supportive book can help the newly diagnosed cancer patient ask better questions, understand there are alternative and integrated treatments that can work and, most of all, maintain hope.

Choices Magazine
Choices is an international online quarterly magazine designed to encourage you to make the right choices and live successful lives. If you have ever felt that you were created for "something more," but just didn't know what or where to start, this publication is for you. It features articles on ways to make your life work. Sign up to receive your complimentary subscription. www.judimoreo.com

Turn Your Speaking Into Cash Order Form

To order additional copies of this book for $24.95 each + shipping/handling, please complete the form below.

Email orders: judi@judimoreo.com

Telephone orders: +1-702-283-4567
Please have your credit card ready.

Postal orders: Turning Point International
3315 E. Russell Road, Ste. A4-404
Las Vegas, Nevada 89120
USA

See our website www.judimoreo.com for FREE information on: Other books, *Choices* magazine, Speaking/Seminars, Consulting

Name: _____

Address: _____

City: _____

State/Province: _____ Postal Code: _____

Telephone: _____

Email: _____

Sales Tax: _____

Shipping by air: _____

Payment Type: ☐ Check   ☐ Credit Card (Visa, MasterCard, AMEX)

Card Number: _____

Name on Card: _____

Expiration Date: _____ / _____   Billing Zip Code: _____

www.ingramcontent.com/pod-product-compliance
Lightning Source LLC
Chambersburg PA
CBHW070735020526
44118CB00035B/1365